The Spirit Who Will Not Be Tamed

The Wesleyan Message and The Charismatic Experience

by Edmund W. Robb

THE SPIRIT WHO WILL NOT BE TAMED
The Wesleyan Message and the Charismatic Experience

© 1997 by Edmund W. Robb
Published by Bristol Books, an imprint of Bristol House, Ltd.

First Edition, May 1997

Unless otherwise indicated, all Scripture quotations are from the *Holy Bible, New International Version,* © 1973, 1978, 1984 by the International Bible Society. Used by permission of Zondervan Publishing House.

ISBN: 1-885224-12-5

Printed in the United States of America

Bristol House, Ltd.
P.O. Box 4020
Anderson, Indiana 46013-4020
Phone: 765-644-0856
Fax: 765-622-1045

To order call: 1-800-451-READ (7323)

To My Daughter Laurie

A

Courageous Witness For Christ

Veni, Creator Spiritus

Come, Holy Ghost, our souls inspire,
    And lighten with celestial fire.
Thou the anointing Spirit art,
    Who dost thy sevenfold gifts impart.
Thy blessed unction from above
    Is comfort, life, and fire of love.
Enable with perpetual light
    The dullness of our blinded sight.
Anoint and cheer our soilèd face
    With the abundance of thy grace.
Keep far our foes; give peace at home;
    Where thou art Guide, no ill can come.
Teach us to know the Father, Son,
    And thee, of both to be but One;
That through the ages all along
    This may be our endless song:
Praise to thy eternal merit,
    Father, Son, and Holy Spirit. Amen.

From the Liturgy for the Ordination of Elders

Acknowledgments

This book is a family affair. My wife, Martha, has typed the manuscript and made many helpful suggestions. Also, she has encouraged me when I was discouraged and tempted to lose heart. Indeed, she is my inspiration.

My son, James Stephen, is a professional editor and journalist. This book would never have been written without his help.

I am grateful to the Directors of The Ed Robb Evangelistic Association for their encouragement and support of this project.

Many of my friends have urged me to write a book about the ministry of the Holy Spirit.

Table of Contents

Preface

I have written this book with a great deal of trepidation. Many of my friends are likely to misunderstand me. Much of the content of this book represents a reevaluation in my thinking. My ministry has been shaped by Wesleyan theology and influenced by the Holiness movement. I have been guilty of many of the prejudices of the traditionalists. Recent events in the church and society, however, have forced me to make an objective study of the ministry and doctrine of the Holy Spirit.

It has been my contention that Wesleyan theology is a mediating expression of the faith. On the right there is Calvinism with its dispensational understanding of the activity of the Holy Spirit. On the left there is Pentecostalism with its excessive subjectivism. The classical Wesleyan position advocates a middle way, anchored in the Word and confirmed in experience. Another way of saying it is, "Christian experience disciplined and informed by the Scriptures."

Wesley, I believe, was an evangelical high churchman. He had a great appreciation for the sacraments as a necessary means of grace and a reverence for tradition. Yet he did not allow his preconceived convictions to inhibit him. He was flexible when it came to spreading the gospel and was willing to reconsider attitudes that were widely held in the Anglican Church. I am convinced that we must follow his example today if we are going to experience renewal.

I have been appalled by how little most United Methodists understand about their historic doctrines. Many have read about Wesley's teachings but few have actually studied what he taught. For instance, there is little understanding of the doctrine of sanctification. It is largely ignored in the contemporary church. Others either make exaggerated claims or minimize the implications. I have tried to record what Wesley actually taught. This represents my understanding and experience.

How can we ignore the Charismatic movement? It is the most dynamic expression of the Christian faith in the world today. To issue a blanket condemnation of a movement that is winning more persons to Christ than any other group is unconscionable. Could God be working positively with a movement that does not always have its theology correct? We don't have to embrace all that some Charismatics or Pentecostals teach to be sympathetic with their devotion and activity.

I have been concerned about church splits. Too often traditionalists feel threatened by a Charismatic presence and therefore make such people unwelcome in the church. Charismatics often are unwise in their zeal and give the impression that they are super-Christians, superior in their faith and experience. Somehow, we must learn to work together. We must remember that "our struggle is not against flesh and blood, but . . . against the powers of this dark world and against the spiritual forces of evil in the heavenly realms" (Ephesians 6:12).

This book has been written with the conviction that a Great Awakening may be about to burst forth. I don't want to miss it. I want my own denomination to be involved, and I am afraid it may be left behind. God forbid.

Edmund W. Robb, Jr.
Lent 1997

CHAPTER 1

Something's Happening in the Church Today

Just in Time to Save Us, Or Is It Too Late?

*A*ny astute observer of the Church today certainly must be struck by the amazing things happening all around the world. Obviously, something very big is going on. But what is it? And, more importantly, how are we to judge it? If it's a good thing, how can we participate while keeping our integrity?

What I'm writing about, of course, is the explosion of Charismatic and Pentecostal churches, both in numbers of churches and in numbers of adherents.

In 1982, world-renowned mission expert David Barrett, together with the Oxford University Press, published the monumental World Christian Encyclopedia, the most complete survey of Christianity and other world religions ever attempted.[1] In his encyclopedia, Barrett reported that in 1980 Pentecostals and Charismatics numbered an estimated 100 million world-wide.

What Barrett revealed was astonishing at the time. To the surprise of many, the largest Protestant church family in the world in 1980 was no longer the Reformation churches such as the Lutherans, Anglicans, Presbyterians, or Baptists, with their 500 years of history. No, the largest family of churches was the Pentecostals, whose churches had begun only 80 years before.

Citing new research, Barrett later reported that by 1985 the number of Charismatics and Pentecostals had jumped to about 150 million. If true, this represents a 50 percent increase in just five years! Astounding! By 1992, only seven years later, the number of Pentecostal and mainline Charismatics had more than doubled, increasing this time to 410,626,000. And it seems to be no accident. Recent estimates indicate that possibly 80 percent of all conversions from paganism now come as a result of Pentecostal or Charismatic ministries.

When the words *Charismatic* or *Pentecostal* are used, many people think only of separate denominations such as the Assemblies of God. Yet millions of Charismatics have never left their mainline churches. This is true of literally every denomination. Consider the Episcopalians, a denomination many consider to be hopelessly stuffy. Former Episcopal Renewal Ministries co-ordinator Charles Iris says 35 of the 149 active Episcopal bishops are actually Charismatic. He adds that 3,000 of the 13,733 Episcopal parish priests are also Charismatic, as are 18 percent of the laity.

Similarly, there is hardly a country in the world without a thriving Pentecostal presence. The famous "house churches" of Communist China are largely Charismatic in their emphasis. The fast-growing Methodist Church of Korea, often cited by American United Methodist evangelicals, is infused with Charismatic zeal. In Africa, Pentecostal preaching is winning people away from tribal religion. And in South America, Pentecostal denominations like the Assemblies of God are converting nominal, non-participating Catholics and turning their lives—and countries—upside down.

Christian programming on the airwaves of the U.S. tends to be heavily Charismatic. Take a minute to list all the televangelists you can think of, and consider how many of them are actually Pentecostals or Charismatics. Although the Christian publishing industry has tended to be dominated by publishers with Reformed connections like Zondervan, many of its best-selling authors have been Charismatic. Think of Benny Hinn, Frank Perretti, and many others.

Yes, it's obvious something very big is happening. While we United Methodists have concentrated nearly all our attention on the impressive advances of the Southern Baptists and the leftward political lurches of groups like the National Council of Churches, the real action has been in those churches where people do odd things like sing contemporary praise choruses, feature live bands during services, raise their hands, and, in many places, speak in unknown tongues.

The explosion of Pentecostalism in this century is a big thing, but is it a good thing? This question cannot be quickly answered. The question itself has several parts, all of which must be answered before judgment can be made. These sub-questions include:

- What exactly is Pentecostalism, and where did it come from?
- How does Pentecostal teaching match up with that of Methodism's founder, John Wesley?
- Have any of the strange phenomena associated with Pentecostalism (shaking, laughing, fainting) been seen in earlier, more generally accepted spiritual movements?
- Could the Pentecostal movement be seen as some sort of Third Great Awakening, or is it more like the founding of a new denomination?
- What about the brand-new movements, such as the "Toronto Blessing," which we've been reading about? Are they authentic?

- What can we learn from Pentecostalism? What might they learn from non-Pentecostals?
- Finally, is The United Methodist Church now "immune" to spiritual awakening? Would a move of the Spirit split us apart, just like the wine skins in the parable?

It Came Out of Nowhere

The Pentecostal revival began at the turn of the century in "Holiness" prayer meetings with groups that had a Wesleyan heritage.[2] As a result of this awakening several new denominations were formed. They include the Assemblies of God, the Foursquare Gospel Church, Pentecostal Holiness Church, the Church of God in Christ, the United Pentecostal Church and the Church of God (Cleveland, Tennessee). The Assemblies of God is presently the fastest growing major Protestant denomination in America. The beginnings of these churches will be explored in chapter seven.

Another impressive expression of this awakening is the growth of the independent Charismatic churches.[3] In almost every city there are congregations that number in the thousands. I know of one city where an independent Charismatic church grew from fewer than 100 to more than 4,000 in ten years. Over the same period every United Methodist congregation in that city declined in membership.

The Pentecostal and Charismatic churches are attracting young people and young adults in growing numbers. The membership of the mainline denominations, without exception on the denominational level, is growing older and declining in vitality. Congregations exhibit little evangelistic zeal or excitement. They are culturally captive to the 1940s and 1950s. The Charismatic congregations, however, have contemporary forms of worship that are relevant to modern Christians.

There is evidence of the Charismatic movement in many United Methodist congregations. Often there is a prayer group.

Sometimes there is a Sunday school class. Occasionally there is a pastor who openly proclaims that he or she is a "Spirit-filled" person. When there is an openness to the Holy Spirit there is vitality and outreach. Too often there is resistance and division. I am afraid that many good Christians who have experienced "the baptism of the Holy Spirit" have felt rejected and have left their denomination. If our church leadership continues to be closed to the movement of the Spirit we shall see an acceleration of this exodus. And we shall be poorer because of it.

It is ironic that there is sometimes more openness to the Charismatic movement in the Roman Catholic Church than there is in United Methodism. That movement has found official acceptance in that most traditional of church bodies. Pope John Paul II has commended the renewal to Catholic priests, and the International Catholic Charismatic Renewal Office occupies an office in the Vatican.

Charismatic renewal is at the heart of the Catholic Church, says Michael Scanlan, president of the University of Steubenville. Scanlan says supernatural healing has become more popular. Songs originating from the renewal have become a regular part of Sunday morning worship for millions of Catholics.

"Evangelical language has become accepted in the Catholic Church through Charismatic renewal," he says. "Catholics talk of having a personal relationship with the Lord. Our students carry around Bibles all the time. On this campus, altar calls are normal."[4] Praise the Lord!

In the mission fields of the world supernatural signs and wonders have been an effective component in world evangelization. This is especially true in Brazil, Chile, and South Korea. When Pope John Paul II first visited Argentina in 1982, only one percent of the population was reportedly Protestant. When he returned in 1995, that number had grown to 25 percent—mostly Pentecostals! A 25-fold increase in only 13 years!

Indeed, it appears that Pentecostal denominations are the largest Protestant churches throughout Latin America. More amazing, I am told that more persons now worship in Assemblies of God churches each Sunday in Brazil than in Roman Catholic churches.

What Accounts for the Growth of the Charismatic and Pentecostal churches?

Before we explore the history of the Pentecostal movement and of other Holy Spirit movements derived largely from the Wesleyan tradition, I want to share some of the conclusions I have reached after years of studying these movements. More to the point, we'll discuss why Pentecostal churches are doing so well while even evangelical mainline congregations are too often stagnating or dying.

They emphasize personal experience

A formal dry religion that does not bring persons to an assurance of salvation and the reality of God in their lives will not have power to attract nor inspire. Individuals feel a sense of alienation, guilt, meaninglessness, and lostness. Mainline churches have been trying to save the world without saving persons. They have been trying to bring in the kingdom through ethical teaching and political efforts rather than bringing lost people to a saving experience in Jesus Christ.

They expect supernatural manifestations and power

For them this is not a closed mechanical universe. They believe in the power of prayer and expect miracles by a sovereign God. The Pentecostals are convinced of the imminent personal return of Jesus Christ. It is not abnormal for them to have healing services; they often witness miraculous healings. They believe that God is active in this world and that his providence is a reality. I will look carefully and critically at some Pentecostal manifestations in this book. But I want to affirm that Christianity is a supernatural religion that stresses the healthful power of God.

They are absolutely convinced that the Bible is the authoritative written Word of God

From their pulpits one hears the prophet proclaim, "Thus saith the Lord." Charismatics are not haunted by their doubts but proclaim their convictions. The traditional mainline scholar may consider them naive and anti-intellectual but they have experienced life-changing power. Mainline church evangelicals often seem less than convinced about the Bible's authority, but Pentecostals rarely display that fault. As the liberal churches decline, the Charismatics preach the sure Word of God to growing congregations.

Their worship services are vital and relevant

Contemporary music is often used. The sermons are not abstract essays, but messages that can clearly be understood and applied. There is a place for witness, prayer and the gifts of the Spirit in their worship. When Charismatics go to worship they are not retreating to some nineteenth-century experience but expressing their faith in a manner that is not foreign to contemporary life.

There is a discipline of life style

Liberal churches are fighting for dubious goals like nonsexist language and acceptance of homosexuality as a valid alternate Christian life style. Liberals also spend much time preaching against vague evils such as ageism and militarism. Yet while they are spellbound with these broad issues their members are often losing the battle with alcohol, divorce, and personal morality. The Pentecostals are proclaiming deliverance from drugs, alcohol, and all manner of personal sins. Homes are being restored and homosexuals and heterosexuals are being saved and changed.

While mainline churches preach racial justice it is the "Spirit-filled" churches that are most likely to be integrated and experiencing brotherhood. The liberal churches proclaim economic justice from the middle-class suburbs but the Pentecostal churches are in the ghetto working with the poor—they see them elevated by the gospel of Christ.

They are not sexist

I have observed another thing in distinctively Charismatic churches. They are not sexist. These congregations recognize that in Christ, "there is neither . . . male nor female, for you are all one in Christ Jesus" (Galatians 3:28). For them the prophecy has been fulfilled: "I will pour out my Spirit on all people. Your sons and daughters will prophesy . . ." (Joel 2:28). Their women have not been enamored of secular feminism because they are free for ministry and service in Jesus Christ. They recognize that this freedom is found in biblical roles and models rather than in competitiveness with men.

Wesleyan Theology Teaches the Holiness of Life

Wesleyan theology teaches us that the evidence of the Spirit-filled life is holiness, and power for witness and service. This expression of the Christian faith is known for its ethical emphasis and theological depth. The "fruit of the Spirit" has been stressed. Unfortunately, the "gifts of the Spirit" have often been neglected or denied by Wesleyan Christians in the twentieth century. Some Methodists have borrowed a page from the dispensationalist book of dogma to teach that the gifts of the Spirit were only for the apostolic age.

The emphasis on holiness has often led to legalism and the glorification of nineteenth-century culture. Too often the Holiness movement retreated to the camp meeting and the rural areas. These problems will be addressed elsewhere in this book.

We desperately need a synthesis of Wesleyan theology and the Charismatic experience. We need the theological depth and ethical emphasis of the Holiness movement and we need the excitement, zeal, freedom, and contemporary expressions of the Charismatics. If we can ever get these two expressions of Wesleyan Christianity united, there is no limit to what might be done.

The gifts of the Spirit are valid today and holiness of life is a necessary evidence of the Spirit-filled life. This emphasis must be affirmed and the discipline of the Scriptures sought.

Of course, little reform will be possible without the cooperation of our pastors. United Methodist and other mainline ministers have been taught very little about the Holy Spirit in their training. This educational breakdown shows in our spiritually impoverished churches. In fact, most aspects of Wesleyan theology were largely neglected in our seminaries until recently. There is now a renewed interest in Wesley and his teachings. Perhaps we shall return to our roots.

There is a major difference that must be reconciled. Charismatics teach a crisis experience of the "baptism of the Holy Spirit." Some Wesleyans teach that all Christians are baptized with the Spirit in the new birth (conversion). It seems that Mr. Wesley taught a definite second work of grace that usually came in a crisis experience but could be gradual.[5]

I will be reviewing the Wesleyan doctrine of the Holy Spirit in chapters two and three. One key conclusion: all Christians have received the Holy Spirit at conversion (1 Corinthians 12:3, 1 Corinthians 3:16), but all believers have not been filled with the Spirit (Ephesians 5:18). This experience of the Holy Spirit may be called a baptism, the Spirit's fullness, or by some other term. This is semantics. The important thing is to open our lives completely and be Spirit-controlled persons. This is the secret of the victorious Christian life and renewal in the church.

I have not been identified with the Charismatic movement. Although I affirm the validity of the gifts of the Spirit, I have never received the gift of tongues. But I believe the Lord has given me the gift of discernment. And I discern that the Spirit is moving today in a unique manner.

The church had better be open!

Are We Seeing 'The Third Wave?'

I want to be part of what Peter Wagner, Professor of Church Growth at Fuller Theological Seminary, has dubbed, "The Third Wave."[6] The first wave of the Holy Spirit moving in this century came around the year 1900, when the Holy Spirit broke through with the humble. The creation of the Pentecostal movement was the result. In the second wave, during the 1960s, he broke through with the spiritually hungry in mainline denominations, with the formation of the Charismatic movement. The Holy Spirit is seeking to break through the denominational barriers of pride and power today to bring a third wave—the third great awakening to America and the world.

As Wagner sees it, in the third wave the Holy Spirit will empower his church and baptize (fill) believers. The emphasis will be on the fruit of the Spirit but with a recognition of the gifts. A Christian's relationship to the Lord will not be judged by the gift he or she receives, but by the spirit of holiness and the endowment of power. Denominational barriers will be overcome, and we shall be one in Christ. The great passion of the church shall be for the souls of lost men and women.

Christians will have an appreciation for the historic liturgy and hymns of the church and yet be free in the Spirit with contemporary expressions of faith and music. Once again the primary task of the church will be the evangelization of the world.

Isn't that the kind of church you would want to belong to? I know I would.

A revived church shall be prepared for the coming of its Lord. Even so, come, Lord Jesus!

Notes

1   *World Christian Encyclopedia,* edited by David B. Barrett (Oxford University Press: Oxford, England, 1982).

2   Peter Hocken, *The Glory and the Shame: Reflections on the 20th Century Outpouring of the Holy Spirit* (Guildford, Surrey, UK: Eagle, 1994), pp. 30–33.

3   Ibid., p. 34.

4   *Challenge to Evangelism Today* (a newsletter published by the Ed Robb Evangelistic Association, Marshall, Texas), "Third Wave," Vol. 19, No. 1, p. 4.

5   Thomas Jackson, ed., *The Works of John Wesley* (1831; reprint, Grand Rapids: Zondervan, n.d.); Sermon 43, "The Scripture Way of Salvation," VI:3:18; Sermon 83, "On Patience," VI:3:11; *A Plain Account of Christian Perfection,* Section 25, Questions 25, XI:423; Letter to Miss Furly, Sept. 15, 1762, XII:207; Letter to a Member of the Society, June 27, 1760, XII:275; Letter to Mrs. A. F., Oct. 12, 1764, XII:333.

6   C. Peter Wagner, *The Third Wave Of The Holy Spirit : Encountering The Power Of Signs And Wonders Today* (Ann Arbor: Servant Publication/Vine Books, 1988).

CHAPTER 2

John Wesley—Holy Spirit Revolutionary

What Methodism's Founder Believed about the Holy Spirit and How That Theology Shook Things Up

*I*f the church is going to be involved in the new wave of Holy Spirit-led renewal we must return to Wesleyan theology, with its evangelical emphasis. Perhaps this sounds strange—looking back to history to get our direction for moving into the future. And yet, John Wesley was an original thinker whose ideas directly or indirectly inspired most renewal movements of the last 250 years. You could almost say Wesley was the original Charismatic. At least, he certainly came off that way to people of his own day.

An Unlikely Revolutionary

John Wesley, during his long, long life, popularized many concepts which can only be described as revolutionary. Being "born again" and getting "sanctified by the Spirit" were ideas first popularized in the English-speaking world by Methodism's founder. Nevertheless, it would be hard to imagine a more unlikely firebrand.

The son of a minister, John Wesley was a highly educated intellectual. He received his Master's in theology at Oxford. He read Greek and Latin proficiently. He kept a personal diary in a secret code so complex that it took 200 years for anyone to crack it. In a day when books were expensive and fewer in number, Wesley read thousands, and not all of them on theology. His lively interest in medicine, for example, led him to write a book of home remedies which went through numerous editions.

John Wesley certainly was not a radical in any conventional sense. Like his father and brother Charles, John Wesley was loyal to the Church of England and did everything in his power to keep Methodism *within* the mother church. Nonetheless, his strong convictions forced him to defy bishops routinely, which pained him. In politics, he was a Tory—a conservative. He backed the King in opposing American independence.

It is also fair to say the young priest was somewhat stiff in his personality—certainly he failed to understand women. His various awkward attempts at romance were for the most part disasters, including his marriage.

By rights, the man who would turn the religious world on its head should have possessed a magnetic personality, should have had an electrifying preaching style, and perhaps have come from a working-class background. But he had none of these. Instead, he was a cautious, conservative Oxford scholar who happened to possess immense courage, a highly original mind, and tremendous organizing skills. God used these gifts to profoundly affect the Christian church.

The thing that made Wesley revolutionary was the amazing contrast between what he was teaching and what was commonly believed 250 years ago. A little background will help set the scene. In the hundred years prior to Wesley, in the seventeenth century, England underwent a terrible civil war, touched off in part by religious differences. In fact, Europe had suffered a series of horrible wars in the seventeenth century between religious factions who were trying to settle theological differences on the battlefield.

So it's no wonder that a great reaction had set in by the turn of the eighteenth century, when Wesley came along. It was considered unfashionable among the educated classes to hold firm spiritual convictions of any kind. This apathy and practical disbelief went all the way up to the Church of England's bishops. They sneered at the early Methodists and their talk of spiritual rebirth, sanctification, supernatural healing, and so forth.

Does any of this sound familiar today?

What Wesley Taught

Let us consider some of the chief characteristics of the Wesleyan message.

All of Wesleyan theology presumes that God is sovereign. That is, God exists, he rules the universe, and he intervenes directly and regularly in the affairs of humans for our good and to further his sovereign purposes.

Secular philosophy (and much liberal theology) has emphasized the freedom of humankind. Humanists contend that humanity determines its own destiny. Secularists believe that history is solely the result of human effort and random cosmic forces. Yet another group believes that some sort of divine being made the world but does not directly run it today. In Wesley's day these persons were known as *deists*.

There was no place in deism for miracles or the supernatural. Many early American leaders such as Ben Franklin and Thomas Jefferson were deists. Deists believed that God created the world, wound it up as though it were an eight-day clock and then left it to its own designs. To them God was an absentee landlord.

I am afraid that there are many practical deists in the church today. Although they may accept church doctrine intellectually, in practice they do not expect God to act in this world. They question the miraculous, deny divine healing, and consider the "witness of the Spirit" (Wesley's term for inner assurance after a spiritual experience which confirms that God has saved you) as fanatical enthusiasm. These kinds of attitudes are the result of a pseudo-intellectualism that is unattractive and a good works salvation that is not biblical.

So, Wesley built his theology on his belief that God really is active in this world.

The Providence of God

Wesleyan Christians believe in the providence of God. We affirm that God is active in this world and his deeds are not limited to known natural law. God is free and transcends our understanding.

Because God is sovereign (transcendent) and imminent (present in this world) the followers of Wesley believe that God continues to speak to his children and manifest his power. We dare not try to limit God.

If God is sovereign his will shall ultimately be done. Christians are on the winning side. "Though the wrong seems oft so strong, / God is the ruler yet," states Malbie Babcock.[1] "Surely the wrath of man shall praise thee" (Psalm 76:10, KJV). Even humanity's rebellion can be made to serve God's plan.

History is moving toward a climax. His will shall ultimately be done with the return of Jesus Christ (John 14:3). "[A]t the name of Jesus every knee should bow . . . and every tongue confess that Jesus Christ is Lord" (Philippians 2:10–11).

Special Providence

A special providence also is manifested in God's concern for persons. This means that although the heavenly Father is concerned about humanity in general, he is also mindful of each human in particular. The Psalmist testified, "The Lord is *my* shepherd . . ."(Psalm 23:1). There is a personal involvement of God in individual lives. "For he will command his angels concerning you to guard you in all your ways," the Bible promises (Psalm 91:11). Every person is important to God. There is a purpose, a plan for every life. Just as every fingerprint is different, so every individual is unique, and uniquely important to God.

God is bringing events together to *enable* people to do his will. He will not force anyone to obey, but he will bring circumstances to bear to bring one to a place of decision and provide grace to enable them to say "yes" to his will.

The first and most important decision a person must make concerning God is to turn his or her life over to the Lord. Humans cannot possibly muster the wisdom to find God. Fortunately, we don't have to, for God finds us. We don't discover the path to God, we are led to him by the Holy Spirit.

Bishop William Cannon's book *The Theology of John Wesley* contains a chapter entitled "Within a Hair's Breadth of Calvinism."[2] Bishop Cannon emphasizes a unique premise of Wesleyan theology. God is sovereign, but humanity is free. Though he wants all persons to be saved, God allows persons to make their own decisions. Persons are responsible for their destiny, but God is very much involved all along the way, always working to give sinners chance after chance to lay down their sin and follow him.

Personal Witness

A story from my life illustrates what I mean.

From early childhood I felt the Holy Spirit wooing and convicting me. It seems that I always had a hunger for God. But as a teenager I strayed from the kingdom. However, even in my worst days of rebellion I knew that if I ever "got right" with God I would preach the gospel. It was always in the back of my mind.

When I was seventeen I joined the Navy. It was 1943 and World War II was raging at the height of its fury. After boot camp and signal school I served in the southwest Pacific. On August 14, 1945, my ship sailed under the Golden Gate bridge in San Francisco Bay, returning to the States after months overseas. It was the day the Japanese announced their unconditional surrender. Three days later I received a 30-day leave with three days' travel time. At the end of my leave I reported to the Naval Induction Center in Dallas, Texas. They had lost my papers. They didn't know what to do with me so they sent me back home on so-called temporary duty. I was home 48 more days. Finally, I received a telegram ordering me to report to Dallas and was sent to Shoemaker, California.

After a few days I was on a draft to go on a battleship for overseas duty. But again they lost my papers, so my orders had to be canceled. A short time later I was on a draft to go to Guam. This time I was in a sick bay with a sore throat, so the doctor scratched me from the list. Finally, I was on a draft for the Market Street Annex, a temporary barracks in downtown San Francisco. I had an easy duty as a Master-At-Arms.

On the weekend of February 1, 1946, I had planned a big outing with a friend who was stationed in Oakland. About six years later, my friend wrote to me with his thoughts concerning that weekend:

> I believe that even today God moves in a mysterious way to help us. You may not recognize it at the time but later you will see it all. I hate to bring up unpleasant memories of the sinful past, but this begins in San Francisco. Remember that "hot" weekend we had planned (hot for hell's fire). My liberty was canceled and I was put on night duty. I know you remember because you went to church that Sunday and were converted.

That's the way it was.

I have never believed it was an accident that I was in that place at that time to hear that particular message. In God's providence he brought me to the place where I could say "yes." The day I was converted I also answered the call to preach the gospel. It was God's plan from the beginning that I should be a preacher. Yes, I could have said "no," but I am convinced that I would have been miserable the rest of my life outside of God's will.

Prevenient Grace

John Wesley taught the doctrine of "prevenient grace." The word *prevenient* means going before or preparing. Our Calvinist friends argue that our salvation cannot possibly be affected by any decision *we* make. If it did, they reason, it would be our *decision for God* rather than *God himself* who saves us. Mr. Wesley contended that prevenient grace enables us to respond to God's call. He cited this biblical passage: "Therefore, my dear friends . . . continue to work out your salvation with fear and trembling, for it is God who works in you to will and to act according to his good purpose" (Philippians 2:12–13). The meaning of these words are made more understandable by transposing them: "It is God that according to his good purpose works in you to will and to act." According to Wesley:

> This position of the words, connecting the phrase, *of his good pleasure*, with the word *worketh*, removes all imagination of the merit from man, and gives God the whole glory of his work. Otherwise, we might have had some room for boasting, as if it were our own dessert, some goodness in us, or some good thing done by us, which first moved God to work.[3]

Ephesians 2:8–9 is another text that teaches prevenient grace. "For it is by grace you have been saved, through faith—and this not from yourselves, it is the gift of God—not by works, so that no one can boast." Not only is grace a gift but faith itself is also a gift of God. Our responsibility is to *exercise* the faith that is given. According to Wesley, no one sins because he or she does not possess enough grace. Rather, that person does not rely on the grace which he or she has.

God gives every individual prevenient grace. It is our responsibility to respond. Saint Augustine has written, "He that made us without ourselves, will not save us without ourselves." This means that although we cannot save ourselves in any way, we do *participate* in God's rescue of our souls.

Evangelist Mark Rutland related a story of prevenient grace in his book, *Launch Out Into the Deep.* He was leading a seminar on winning people to Christ in Atlanta, and all the participants were given the assignment of going out in teams to share the good news. Although Mark tried to follow God's direction, he and his partner of the afternoon had enjoyed no success. On the way back to the conference center, they passed a very shabby white house with junk surrounding it.

Driving by in their car, Mark felt the Holy Spirit speaking with urgency, "Go in that house, and I will give you a soul." At first he ignored the voice and drove on, but the Spirit was insistent, and finally he asked his partner to turn the car around. They walked up to the house, went around to the side, and were greeted by—a motorcycle gang! These dangerous-looking, dirty young men and a few young women just glared at the evangelism team menacingly. One had a blue tattoo reading, "BORN TO KILL." Mark says he thought, "Lord, I hope it's not me."

Feeling the Lord wanted him to deliver his message anyway, Mark's nervousness translated into immediate action. He virtually erupted into preaching God's plan of salvation with no small talk beforehand. This spectacle apparently stunned the gang, for they just waited in open-mouthed silence for this strange man to finish whatever he was saying. After giving his lightning-fast message, Mark asked the dumbfounded group if they wanted to accept Christ as Savior. No one said anything. Feeling sure the Lord had prepared someone, he went around the group and asked each one individually. Did they want to receive Jesus into their hearts? Each shook his or her head "no," and Mark and his friend began their retreat toward the car, with Mark feeling he had misunderstood the Spirit's command. And then:

> Just as Bill and I turned toward the car we heard a voice. It was that of a child.
>
> "Wait a minute, Mister," said the voice.
>
> Behind the big choppers, well out of our view was a table covered with a filthy sheet of canvas that draped to the floor forming a tent-like structure. From his den there, a lad of about 10 or 11 had listened to the whole thing, undetected by Bill and me and ignored by the adults. He crawled out wearing only a pair of khaki cut-offs.
>
> "Wait a minute," he repeated as I turned back to him. "I want Jesus to come into *my* heart." His scrawny, nearly naked little body gave him the look of a Dickens pick-pocket, but his dirty face was as guileless as Billy Budd.[4]

Right there Mark and the boy dropped to their knees, and the child accepted Christ in the midst of the amazed gang members. What are the chances that a boy in an atmosphere like that would have been able to hear the Gospel message? Yet God did not wait to be "discovered" by this lad. God discovered him and prepared him to receive Christ. That is prevenient grace at work.

The Protection of God in Context

Providence implies protection. No permanent harm can come to the person who is in God's will. That does not mean that everything that happens to a person is God's will and is for the best. We can and will lose even our own lives, yet God's grace follows us even beyond the grave. As the Scripture promises, "in all things God works for the good of those who love him, who have been called according to his purpose" (Romans 8:28). This verse is sometimes misinterpreted to mean that all things are for the "best" for Christians. No, but it does mean that God is with the believer in every situation and good will come out of it as we trust him.

People sometimes say, "Bad things happen to good people!" But out of the trials of life good things can come. God does not *cause* all things, but he can bring good things out of the bad and use all things to his glory.

The Hand of God

John Wesley, in his sermon, "Spiritual Worship," teaches a unique understanding of providence. Although Methodism's founder wrote more than 200 years ago, and thus may be a little difficult to read, his meaning is clear:

> [T]here is a difference . . . in [God's] providential government over the children of men. A pious writer observes, There is a three-fold circle of divine providence. The *outermost circle* includes all the sons of men; Heathens, Mahometans [Moslems], Jews, and Christians. He causeth his sun to rise upon all. He giveth them rain and fruitful seasons. He pours ten thousand benefits upon them, and fills their hearts with food and gladness. With an *interior circle* he encompasses the whole visible Christian Church, all that name the name of Christ. He has an additional regard to these, and a nearer attention to their welfare. But the *innermost circle* of his providence encloses only the invisible Church of Christ; all real Christians, wherever dispersed in all corners of the earth; all that worship God (whatever denomination they are of) in spirit and in truth. He keeps these as the apple of an eye: He hides them under the shadow of his wings. And it is to these in particular that our Lord says, "Even the hairs of your head are all numbered."[5]

It was in December of 1987 and I was hunting quail in West Texas. I was accidentally shot. Over one hundred pellets from the shotgun blast entered my body. Some pellets entered in the back of my head, neck, shoulder and arm. I was flown by a Lear jet hospital plane from Wichita Falls to Houston. The first thing they asked at the hospital was whether I was an organ transplant donor—they assumed I would soon die. In fact, a shot grazed one of my carotid arteries. Had it punctured the artery, I would not even have made it to the hospital. And yet, amazingly, I was not killed.

However, for months I did not have use of my right arm or hand. I had to learn to write and eat my meals with my left hand. For several weeks I was in constant, almost unbearable pain. Today I have the complete use of my arm and hand and the pain is gone. The Lord did not cause me to be shot. It was an unfortunate accident. But he has used that experience for his glory. Perhaps he nudged some of the pellets and caused them to miss a vital organ. In his providence I am convinced he saved my life for a purpose.

Through the eyes of faith all committed Christians should see the hand of God. We must learn to look at life through the eyes of faith. It is by his providence that we are here. Providence implies provision. The promise of the Bible is, "my God will meet all your needs according to his glorious riches in Christ Jesus" (Philippians 4:19). I have noticed that provision is related to prayer. "You do not have, because you do not ask God" (James 4:2). Jesus said, "Ask and it will be given you; seek and you will find; knock and the door will be opened to you" (Matthew 7:7). On another occasion he said, "whatever you ask for in prayer, believe that you have received it, and it will be yours" (Mark 11:24).

He will provide for us financially. It was 1950. I had just been appointed pastor of a small church in West Texas. My wife Martha and I had two babies and no food. I was inexperienced and did not know what to do. I believe my salary was $250 a month! It was before I had learned to borrow money from a bank. We were new in town and didn't know anyone well enough to tell them our dilemma.

In desperation one morning Martha and I got on our knees and poured out our hearts to God. We prayed something like this, "Lord we are trying to serve you. We are doing the best we know how. We don't know what to do or where to turn. We are trusting in you to meet our need." We prayed this prayer about 8:30 a.m. It must have been 10:00 a.m. when we heard a knock at the door. It was one of our faithful members. She said, "Brother Robb, I felt impressed this morning to bring this gift to you. This is not for the church but for you and Martha." It was like manna from heaven and an answer to prayer. She had given me a $20 bill. Some would say that was a coincidence. Don't you believe it!

Several weeks later we were facing another financial crisis. I had borrowed $10 from a loan shark company. At the end of the month, I could only pay the interest, $2.40! We had no milk for the babies. We again got on our knees at the very same place we had prayed before and asked in faith that God would provide for our need. That very afternoon, a young college boy knocked on my door. I had never seen him before. He asked, "Are you Brother Robb?" I said, "Yes," and he gave me $40 and left with no explanation. I have no doubt but that this was an answer to prayer. The Psalmist said, "I was young and now I am old, yet I have never seen the righteous forsaken or their children begging bread" (Psalm 37:25).

The Lord Heals

Providence implies that the Lord provides for our healing. We are instructed by the Apostle James, "Is any one of you sick? He should call the elders of the church to pray over him and anoint him with oil in the name of the Lord. And the prayer offered in faith will make the sick person well; the Lord will raise him up" (James 5:14–15).

Following my hunting accident, as I have said, I experienced terrible pain in my right arm and hand for several months. I was desperate, and for a period of time a cloud was over me day and night. Everyone who has suffered chronic pain will know what I mean. It was the worst experience of my life.

I was in the Houston area for an appointment with my doctor, so on Sunday I worshipped at The Woodlands United Methodist Church where my son, Edmund III, is the pastor. During the prelude I was looking over the bulletin and found this announcement, "We have a healing team. If you would like to have special prayer for your healing, remain at the chancel following the benediction." I responded to that invitation. The associate pastor, together with a layman and my wife, took me to a small room for prayer. We discussed my problems and then had conversational prayers. As we prayed the cloud of depression was lifted and the joy of my salvation returned.

About that same time an internist recommended to my son that I go to a colleague of his, an anesthesiologist, to get a "sympathetic nerve block." I believe this was the Holy Spirit leading in response to our prayers for healing. After the third treatment the pain left and did not come back. I was healed. For the first time in months I was without pain.

The providence of God includes providing for all of our needs—including healing.

Notes

1 "This is my Father's World."

2 *The Theology of John Wesley*, William R. Cannon (Nashville: Abingdon Press, 1946), p. 8.

3 *Works*, sermon 85, "On Working Out Your Own Salvation," VI: p. 508.

4 Mark Rutland, *Launch Out Into the Deep* (Anderson, Ind.: Bristol Books, 1987), pp. 162–165.

5 *Works*, sermon 77, "Spiritual Worship," VI: 428f..

CHAPTER 3

Radical Teachings on Salvation and the Second Work of Grace

What Wesley Did—and Did Not—Teach about the Holy Spirit

*J*ohn Wesley's greatest departure from the religious leaders of his day was his insistence that individual persons had to be "born again." Of course, Methodism's founder did not invent this concept. All Christians versed in their Bibles know that Jesus told the Pharisee Nicodemus, who came to visit him at night, "unless a man is born again, he cannot see the kingdom of God" (John 3:3).

Although this verse seems plain to most of us today, that is mostly because Wesley and his followers, and others such as George Whitefield, popularized and explained the concept. In the eighteenth century, Anglican theology did teach that the world's salvation came through Christ's work on the cross. Yet most people assumed that the way they could become saved themselves was by being a faithful member of the church, leading a good life, taking the Lord's Supper, and so forth. The personal nature of salvation, that Christ died for *you*, was not stressed. No one talked about being "born again."

Wesley probably wouldn't have, either, except that he had a providential encounter with a group of German Christians known as Moravians during his sojourn to America in 1735. These good people had rediscovered Jesus' teaching on the new birth and were preaching that individuals had to be born again to be saved. The Moravians had errors in their theology, but they did emphasize personal salvation with assurance. This concept immediately appealed to Wesley, for it promised to explain a mystery.

Although Wesley had been a striving, near-fanatical churchman all his life, always fasting, studying, and praying, he had serious doubts about his salvation. Wesley was certainly methodical in his religious approach, but he suspected that his religion was empty. He instinctively knew that something critical was missing. But what was it?

His suspicion was confirmed during the voyage to America aboard the ship *Simmonds.* For three terrifying weeks a storm threatened to rip the vessel apart and send her to the bottom. Wesley, like almost all the others on board, eventually became so frightened that he lost all hope, certain he would soon die. But when he came upon the Moravians, he was amazed to find them all quite calm, praying with confidence. Wesley compared his mental state with theirs and decided he wanted what they had.

What they had was assurance. Within three years John Wesley began his 50-year career of preaching the message, "You must be born again." But as a scholar and careful thinker, he felt the need to explain this experience in a way that made sense intellectually as well as emotionally. He relied on the classical doctrine of justification to give a framework to his thinking.

The doctrine of justification is at the very heart of Wesley's evangelical theology. According to Mr. Wesley, *justification* takes place in the mind of God. *Regeneration* takes place in the hearts of men and women. The former is judicial (God's view of us changes), the latter is experiential (we become different people).

Justification is the great work God does for us, in forgiving our sins; regeneration is the great work which God does in us, in the renewing of our fallen nature. In order of time, neither of these is before the other.[1]

Baptismal Regeneration

Wesleyans have never taught "baptismal regeneration" nor have we ever equated church membership with salvation. Should we be baptized as Christians? Yes. Is baptism a part of the saving process? No. The idea that baptism saves, or that it is absolutely necessary to salvation, is taught by a variety of denominations, and the Methodists of today seem constantly tempted to fall into this error.[2]

Wesleyans do not believe that baptism or the Lord's Supper saves. Rather, God saves us as we give our lives over to him personally, thus experiencing the "new birth." Although baptism and the Lord's Supper do not save, they are means of grace. That is, God does minister to people through these sacraments.

Infant baptism is a celebration of prevenient grace. It is not a ceremony which brings about salvation. Mr. Wesley says it is evident that baptism is only a sign of regeneration (being saved) as distinct from regeneration itself. Baptism is an outward sign of an inward and spiritual grace. Nothing is plainer, says Wesley, than that baptism is not the same as the new birth. One is external, the other an internal work. The one being the act of man, purifying the body, the other a change brought by God in the soul. As Wesley puts it, "Be you baptized or unbaptized, 'you must be born again.'"

Wesley continues,

"Nay, but I constantly attend all the ordinances [sacraments] of God: I keep to my church and sacrament." It is well you do: But all this will not keep you from hell, except you be born again. Go to church twice a day; go to the Lord's table every week; say ever so many prayers in private; hear ever so many good sermons; read ever so many good books; still, "you must be born again." None of these things will stand in the place of the new birth, no, nor any thing under heaven.[3]

In Wesley's view, those who have been born again have been justified. What is justification?

The word *justification* could be translated, "Just as if I had never sinned." By virtue of faith in Christ the sinner stands perfect before God. This is the glorious scriptural doctrine of atonement which could be translated, "At-one-ment." The barriers of sin are broken down through the shed blood of Jesus Christ. "God made him who had no sin to be sin for us, so that we in him might become the righteousness of God" (2 Corinthians 5:21).

"He himself bore our sins in his body on the tree, so that we might die to sins and live for righteousness; by his wounds you have been healed" (1 Peter 2:24). This is called the substitutionary atonement. Literally, Christ became our substitute, taking the punishment we deserved. He took our place.

As Wesleyans we have so emphasized the necessity of living the Christian life that I am afraid we have often failed to present salvation as a definite *gift* of faith. It is not clear in many people's minds that salvation is by grace through faith alone (Ephesians 2:8–9). I am convinced many good church people have no assurance of salvation. The great Methodist missionary E. Stanley Jones often repeated his estimate that no more than one-third of church members had actually been born again.

The Witness of the Spirit

The unique contribution that Methodists have made to Christian theology is the doctrine of the "witness of the Spirit." John Wesley taught us that it was the birthright of every believer not only to be saved but to *know* that he or she is saved.

One of history's great ironies is that some of the most fundamental points of progress are taken for granted, because the new knowledge seems so obvious in retrospect. For example, the knowledge that bacteria exist and can kill you seems obvious today. In Wesley's day, however, the existence of germs was unknown.

It is the same with Wesley's doctrine of the "witness of the Spirit." Today almost every evangelical church in the world teaches that you can know that you are saved. Throughout Christian history there have been those persons so afraid for their souls that they went to gross extremes such as self-mutilation and punishing long fasts. They believed it was impossible to know for sure they were saved, so they just kept working harder and harder.

Thanks be to God! We don't have to fear that we haven't done enough, or that we missed some vital piece of knowledge which could have saved us.

Some question whether this matter of being "saved" is a Methodist doctrine at all. I say that it is one the most fundamental of all Methodist doctrines! It is certainly a biblical doctrine. The prevailing theme from Genesis to Revelation is salvation. We read that the purpose for Christ coming into the world was "to seek and to save what was lost" (Luke 19:10).

But it's one thing to be a believer, and another thing to know you are saved. The great Methodist movement is founded on a very famous experience John Wesley had shortly after returning home in spiritual defeat from Georgia. On May 24, 1738, dejected, Wesley went to a religious society meeting held in London's Aldersgate Street. The rest is history. He recorded the experience in his journal:

> In the evening I went very unwillingly to a society in Aldersgate-Street, where one was reading Luther's preface to the Epistle to the Romans. About a quarter before

nine, while he was describing the change which God works in the heart through faith in Christ, I felt my heart strangely warmed. I felt I did trust in Christ, Christ alone for salvation: And an assurance was given me, that he had taken away *my* sins, even *mine*, and saved *me* from the law of sin and death.[4]

So Methodism was founded on the experience of assurance—the witness of the Spirit. Even after 250 years, theologians still debate whether Wesley was actually born again at Aldersgate, or if he merely received the inward confirmation of his salvation. That point will never be settled. But we do know this—before Aldersgate Wesley was not sure he was a Christian. After Aldersgate, he knew he was. He had been given the witness of the Spirit.

The Scriptures do teach the doctrine of the witness of the Spirit. We read, "The Spirit himself testifies with our spirit that we are God's children" (Romans 8:16). Also, "Anyone who believes in the Son of God has this testimony in his heart" (1 John 5:10).

John and Charles Wesley, along with their brother, Samuel, were standing at the bedside of their dying father. All three sons were ministers in the Church of England. The elderly father gave this testimony as he was about to die. He exclaimed to them, "The witness of the Spirit, the witness of the Spirit, this is the greatest proof of Christianity."

Interestingly this high church priest gave this affirmation long before the Aldersgate experience. It seems clear that God was preparing Wesley to learn and then to spread this much-needed truth throughout England, and from there to all the world.

The Leap of Faith

Many are so close to the kingdom but have never made that "leap of faith" and crossed the goal line.

It was the fall of 1969. My family was living in Abilene, Texas, and our Cooper High School had the greatest team in Texas football history. Our Cooper team won all the games of the regular season easily. The play-off games went well. The final game for the state championship was played at Amon Carter Field in Fort Worth. Everyone predicted our team would win. But when the final whistle blew we were on the one-inch line and two points behind. We had come so close, but we lost.

That is the picture of many persons without Christ. They are in the church but they don't know the Lord of the church. They have been baptized but have not been born again. They are on the one-inch line. They must take the leap of faith and cross the goal line.

Persons Are Lost without Jesus Christ

On one occasion, I was at a radio station recording some devotionals for later airing. In the lobby I noticed a well-known country singer. I felt led to witness to him. He responded, "Ed, I'm not such a bad guy." And the truth is—he was a nice person. But we are not saved by "niceness," we are saved by grace.

Even nice persons are lost without Jesus Christ. We only come to know him through a personal experience of forgiveness and grace—the new birth.

As a society, and even as a church, perhaps we have lost the conviction that persons need Jesus Christ. If none are lost, why should any need to be saved?

I flew into the Cleveland, Ohio, airport. I was scheduled to speak at the East Ohio Evangelical fellowship which was meeting at the United Methodist camp ground on Lake Erie. A friend who was a pilot and navigator for American Airlines met me. I got into his car in perfect confidence, knowing my friend would drive me to my destination. We left Cleveland heading for the camp 60 miles away. Forty-five minutes later I looked up and saw the Cleveland skyline. We had taken the wrong road and circled all the way around that great city. We were lost, and we didn't know it. We were going in circles, and we didn't realize it. We were enjoying the trip—we just didn't know where we were.

That is the picture of persons without Christ. Many are lost, but they don't know it. Some are religious, but do not have the assurance of salvation. They are going in circles, but they are not going to end up where they hope to go.

I am afraid we have lost a sense of the horror and terror of sin. Bishop Arthor J. Moore once said, "In our day we have humanized God, we have deified man and we have minimized sin." God takes sin seriously—not because he is a tyrant who wants to limit us but because he is a heavenly father who wants to protect us. He knows the devastating consequences of sin—broken homes, shattered lives, sick personalities.

Some time ago, after an evening worship service, a young housewife came to me and said, "Ed, you are always saying that a person should be able to say, 'I am saved.'" She added, "That sounds presumptuous to me. It sounds as though you are saying, 'Look how good I am.'" I responded, "You don't understand. When you say that you are a Christian, you are not saying that you are good but rather you are saying, 'Look what a great Savior I have.'" We are not saved by our goodness, but by God's grace.

Salvation Is an Experience—A Relationship

At times I ask a person if he or she is a Christian, and the individual will answer, "Partly." I am inclined to ask them what part of them is going to heaven. Salvation is an experience— one has entered into it or one has not. One could say that salvation is a relationship. You either have it or you don't.

I have also asked persons if they are Christians and they reply, "I'm trying to be." One is not saved by trying, but by trusting. "Therefore, since we have been justified through faith, we have peace with God through our Lord Jesus Christ" (Romans 5:1).

Before Aldersgate, John Wesley had the faith of a servant (i.e., servile, unconfident, beaten down). After Aldersgate, he had the faith of a son (joyful, personal). Too many church members today have a servant relationship with God rather than a personal family relationship.

There are many cultural "Christians" who cannot witness to the assurance of salvation.

The hereditary believer professes to be a second or third generation Christian. "Our family has always been Christian," someone might say. But E. Stanley Jones said it well, "There are no grandchildren in the family of God." There comes a time when your mother's Savior must become your own personal Savior—when your father's Lord must become your Lord.

Persons are fortunate who have a great Christian heritage. But this faith must be appropriated personally. Someone has said that it takes three generations to backslide. The first generation has a vital Christian experience. The second generation has the memory and respects the tradition. The third generation has lost the memory and often the respect.

Which generation are you in?

Sanctification—God Changes Us

Wesley's views on the Holy Spirit were amazingly influential in church history. As shall be shown in later chapters, most of our contemporary Holy Spirit movements have their roots in the teachings of Wesley. Some of these movements have stretched and altered Wesley's doctrines to the breaking point, perhaps, but he is the original influence nonetheless.

Although such ideas as being "baptized in the Spirit" developed from Wesley's teaching, Methodism's founder himself never used this term. Yet he did teach that beyond the new birth, there was another encounter with the Holy Spirit that believers needed to undergo. His term for this experience was "sanctification."

The forgotten word in the worldwide church today is *sanctification*. This is particularly disappointing for those in the Wesleyan tradition, because sanctification was a primary emphasis in the great evangelical revival led by John Wesley in eighteenth-century England. Holiness and assurance were the unique teachings of the people called Methodists.

The word *sanctification* means to be made holy, to consecrate, to set apart for holy purpose, to purify.

The first thing we need to realize in consideration of holiness is that all Christians are sanctified in the eyes of God because of the sacrifice of Christ Jesus. We read in 1 Corinthians 1:30: "It is because of him that you are in Christ Jesus, who has become for us wisdom from God—that is, our righteousness, holiness and redemption."

Thus, the redeemed stand holy (perfect) before God by virtue of the merit of the shed blood of the Savior. This is the judicial aspect of sanctification. The term "sanctified" is applied by St. Paul to all who are justified.

So, Wesley, as he developed his theology, began teaching that all Christians are sanctified—a relatively simple concept. After that, however, things get a bit more difficult to understand. That's because the term *sanctification*, used by itself, rarely if ever means "saved from all sin." By that I mean being sanctified, as all Christians are in the sense described above, does not mean you are immune to committing sins or even desiring to commit them. In other words, though Christians are sanctified in the eyes of God, they may not be sanctified in terms of their own character.

It is not proper to use the term *sanctification* to mean "personally saved from all sin" without adding the word "wholly," "entirely," or the like. The inspired writers of the Bible almost continually speak of those who were justified, but rarely of those who were wholly sanctified. Consequently, Mr. Wesley writes, ". . . it behoves us [is proper] to speak almost continually of the state of justification; but more rarely, at least in full and explicit terms, concerning entire sanctification."[5]

So what result does our justification (being saved) have on our actual character here on earth? When does inward sanctification begin? The answer is that sanctification of the heart begins in the moment a person is justified. From that time a believer should gradually die to sin, and grow in grace.

What Is Christian Perfection?

What is Christian perfection? It is loving God with all our heart, mind, soul, and strength and loving one's neighbor as one's self. This perfection excludes all infirmities, ignorance, and mistakes. Thus, Christian perfection is the perfecting of the heart's desires, rather than one's performance.

Mr. Wesley teaches in his "Brief Thoughts on Christian Perfection:"

(1) By perfection I mean the humble, gentle, patient love of God, and our neighbour, ruling our tempers, words, and actions.

I do not include an impossibility of falling from it, either in part or in whole. . . . And I do not contend for the term *sinless*.

(2) . . . I believe this perfection is always wrought in the soul by a simple act of faith; consequently, in an instant.

But I believe a gradual work, both preceding and following that instant.

(3) As to the time. I believe this instant generally is the instant of death, the moment before the soul leaves the body. But I believe it may be ten, twenty, or forty years before.

I believe it is usually many years after justification; but that it may be within five years or five months after it, I know no conclusive argument to the contrary.[6]

Many things can be learned about Wesley's teaching from the above passage. Obviously, the Anglican priest was not rigid (unlike some of today's Holiness movements). He believed God would make Christians free from sin, but he mentions several different ways this experience may occur:

- It may be instantaneous, or it may take years.
- Although sanctification could be gradual, there was usually a crisis experience you could point to as the key moment of the process. This is what many have called a second work of grace.
- Sanctification could be lost—"fallen from."
- To be sanctified means a perfection of intent rather than deed.

The most usual time God perfects us is at the moment of our deaths. On other occasions Wesley insisted that one should seek entire sanctification in this life.

So Wesley, during his preaching and teaching career, urged people to obtain two vital spiritual experiences. The first was being born again, and the second was being sanctified.

The Roman Catholic Church and his own church, the Church of England, both had a doctrine of sanctification, but neither emphasized it as an experience. This understanding directly paved the way to later ideas such as being "baptized in the Spirit," etc. (In a later chapter we will discuss how the "baptism of the Spirit" developed out of Wesley's teaching.)

Entire Sanctification—What Can This Term Mean?

Entire sanctification does not imply "sinless perfection." This would indicate an inability to sin or a moral perfection that is not attained this side of heaven. Rather, as Wesley saw it, entire sanctification results in Christian perfection. That is, a perfection of intent or desire, not of expression or action, a perfection in love.

Victory Over Sin

The doctrine of entire sanctification contends the believer *can* be victorious over sin. Christians need not be defeated by temptation. A text often used in support of this scriptural truth is, "May God himself, the God of peace, sanctify you through and through. May your whole spirit, soul and body be kept blameless at the coming of our Lord Jesus Christ" (1 Thessalonians 5:23).

It is important to note that although Wesley preached the experience of entire sanctification, he never claimed this experience for himself. Always ruthlessly self-critical and honest, he was hesitant to testify of this experience. But he believed the Bible taught that Christians could be freed and cleansed from sin, so he always emphasized this teaching.

Mr. Wesley described the *experience* of sanctification this way:

> An instantaneous change has been wrought in some believers: None can deny this . . .
> "'But in some this change was not instantaneous.' They did not perceive the instant when it was wrought. It is often difficult to perceive the instant when a man dies; yet there is an instant in which life ceases. And if ever sin ceases, there must be a last moment of its existence, and a first moment of our deliverance from it."[7]

Some reject the doctrine of Christian perfection or entire sanctification because they assume it teaches a static condition— that the sanctified believer has "arrived" morally and spiritually. This certainly is not the case. Just as there is growth before the Spirit-filled life, there continues to be growth after the experience. In fact, that growth should be accelerated.

Social Holiness

Wesley said, "There is no holiness without social holiness." I am afraid that many have so personalized this message that we have neglected the implications of the gospel in society. The Holiness movement (discussed in a later chapter) in the early nineteenth century crusaded against slavery and all kinds of social injustice.

Later, however, in reaction to the "Fundamentalist-Modernist" controversy, this dynamic movement retreated to the camp meetings and the rural areas of the nation. The leadership became associated with reaction and anti-intellectualism. Too often its message was associated with negative feelings about the institutional church. It gradually lost much of its influences and established religious ghettos isolated from the general church and the larger world.

The church and society are poorer because of this. Wesley himself was a tireless social crusader. He worked for better public health, urged employers to pay fair wages, worked to promote public literacy, and much more. In fact, Wesley's last recorded letter was to William Wilberforce commending him for his crusade against slavery in the British Empire.[8]

The church needs the ethical and experiential emphasis of Wesleyan theology and a sinful and rebellious world desperately needs the prophetic voice of Wesleyan preachers. We need to return to our theological roots and reclaim the passion for the kingdom of God.

Wesleyan Christians in the past have been in the forefront of the crusades for education, missions, and social reform.

Do it again Lord, do it again.

Notes

1   Robert Burkner and Robert Chiles, *A Compend of Wesley's Theology* (New York: Abingdon, 1954), pp. 101–102.

2   Wesley's *A Treatise on Baptism* (*Works*, X:188–201) must be interpreted in the light of his other writings.

3   *Works*, Sermon 45, "The New Birth," VI:76–77.

4   *Works*, *Journal*, May 24, 1738, I:103.

5   *Works*, XI:388.

6   Ibid., p. 446.

7   Ibid., p. 442.

8   The letter may be found in *Works*, XIII:153.

CHAPTER 4

Just Who and What Is This Holy Spirit?

The Person and Ministry of the Holy Spirit

*B*efore going further into what the Holy Spirit is doing in the world today, we need to look deeper into who this Spirit is.

Some time ago a friend of mine was playing golf with a pastor. The minister told my friend that his congregation had recently turned a member out of the church for getting drunk. My friend asked how long it had been since they had kicked someone out of the church for not being filled with the Holy Spirit. The same text that forbids Christians to get drunk commands them to be filled with the Spirit (Ephesians 5:18).

As I travel across the church I find that many persons have only a vague idea who the Holy Spirit is and many are not sure they want to know. They are afraid of the possibility of fanaticism.

Yet I believe that the danger in the church today is not fanaticism but spiritual death. The Holy Spirit, rightly understood, should bring balance, spiritual health, and wholeness. It has been said that we cannot go further until we go deeper. If we go deeper we must rediscover the experience and doctrine of the Holy Spirit.

Who Is the Holy Spirit?

Christians believe in one God. This one God has revealed himself in three persons—Father, Son and Holy Spirit. The Son is not the Father, and the Holy Spirit is not the Son. But the Father *is* God, the Son *is* God and the Holy Spirit *is* God. We sing in a familiar hymn "God in three persons, blessed Trinity."

I know many faithful Christians are confused about the Trinity. How can the Father and the Son and the Holy Spirit all be God yet all be distinct personalities at the same time?

The word *trinity* is not found in the Bible, but the truth of the Trinity is revealed throughout Scriptures. The Great Commission witnesses to the reality of this great doctrine. "Therefore go and make disciples of all nations, baptizing them in the name of the Father, and of the Son and of the Holy Spirit" (Matthew 28:19). The Apostolic benediction given by Paul in 2 Corinthians 13:14 testifies to the truth of the Trinity: "May the grace of the Lord Jesus Christ, and the love of God [the Father], and the fellowship of the Holy Spirit be with you all."

The Christian's experience confirms the triune nature of God. All believers know the Father as the Sovereign Lord of history. It is from him that "every good and perfect gift" comes. He is the ruler, sustainer and judge of the universe. It is to the heavenly Father that we normally offer our prayers. All followers of the Way have seen that "God was reconciling the world to himself in Christ . . ." (2 Corinthians 5:19). "He was God as though he were never man, and he was man as though he were never God." All believers have experienced the Holy Spirit. For the Christian, God is not some "Wholly Other" but the God who is experienced and known now through the person of the Holy Spirit.

I use a series of alliterative words to teach the principles of who the Holy Spirit is.

The Holy Spirit Is Promise

The Holy Spirit is the *promise* of the Father. Hundreds of years before the coming of Christ the prophet Joel wrote, "I will pour out my Spirit on all people . . ." (Joel 2:28). You may recall that this prophesy was quoted by Peter when he preached his great sermon on the day of Pentecost (Acts 2:17).

John the Baptist, the forerunner of Jesus and the last of that noble line of Old Testament prophets said, "I baptize you with water for repentance. But after me will come one who is more powerful than I . . . He will baptize you with the Holy Spirit . . ." (Matthew 3:11).

The last words of Jesus recorded in Acts and Luke promised the gift of the Holy Spirit to his disciples (Luke 24:49; Acts 1:5–8).

In the farewell address of our Lord, Jesus assured his disciples that they would receive the Holy Spirit after his ascension (John 14:26, 15:26).

Some argue that the gift of the Holy Spirit was for the Apostolic age and the active presence of the Holy Spirit was withdrawn with the completion of the New Testament. But Peter is recorded as saying, "The promise is for you and your children and for all who are far off—for all whom the Lord our God will call" (Acts 2:39).

The promise is for all the followers of Jesus until the end of the age, and that includes you and me.

The Holy Spirit Is Personal

The Holy Spirit is a *person*. The personal pronoun used in the Greek New Testament in reference to the Holy Spirit is neuter, that is, not gender specific. The early Latin Fathers preferred to use the masculine personal pronoun. But Jesus spoke in the Aramaic, and I am told that he would have used the feminine personal pronoun in speaking of the Holy Spirit.[1] This suggests some interesting insights to us. What do we associate with the feminine spirit? I think of warmth.

Frankly, many Protestant churches are so cold they resemble walk-in refrigerators. Some congregations put so much value upon "restraint" in their church services that it is as though they are worshiping God through a telescope—the Lord seems cold and withdrawn. The Holy Spirit brings the warmth of his presence to us. We associate beauty and color with the feminine spirit. The person of the Holy Spirit brings color to our lives and beauty to our worship. He saves us from drab formality and dead legalism. Certainly warmth, love and beauty should fill the house of God. These are the works of the Holy Spirit.

Another feminine characteristic is emotion. Often evangelical Christians are accused of emotionalism. Generally speaking, the charge is false. To *manipulate* the emotions is wrong and to rely upon them leads to instability. However, a religion without emotion is a sick religion. Anything that is meaningful causes deep feeling. Joy is an emotion. Compassion involves emotion. Love has emotion. To be saved from the deep-seated feeling of guilt certainly should lead to the emotion of praise and thanksgiving.

The Holy Spirit never leads one to manipulate emotions but liberates the suppressed desires and transforms them into Christian joy. This is not "emotionalism" but leads to an outlet of healthful emotion, without which one is a sick person, crippled spiritually and mentally.

The feminine spirit suggests mystery to me. I have been married 50 years. My wife is still a wonderful mystery to me. Many men have expressed the same feeling. Women are different from men and that is part of the attraction. The Christian faith is more than doctrine and rules. We behold a mystery and stand in awe of the triune God.

The Holy Spirit Is the Divine Presence

The Holy Spirit is the Divine *Presence.*[2] The Psalmist expressed the truth of the unique presence of the Holy Spirit when he wrote, "Where can I go from your Spirit? Where can I flee from your presence? If I go up to the heavens, you are there; if I make my bed in the depths, you are there. If I rise on the wings of the dawn, if I settle on the far side of the sea, even there your hand will guide me, your right hand will hold me fast" (Psalms 139:7–10).

I was in Moscow in 1971 during the Cold War. On the first Sunday in January we attended the Baptist Church which was the only Protestant Church in the city at that time. It was bitterly cold on the outside but we felt the warmth of God's presence on the inside. The church was packed with devout believers. Many were standing in the snow outside because there was no room in the sanctuary. We realized that after more than 50 years of persecution and atheistic propaganda under Communist rule the church was very much alive in Soviet Russia. The Iron Curtain couldn't shut God out. My wife and I were in Moscow, but we had never felt the presence of God more. We were not alone.

God the Holy Spirit is found everywhere except in the perverted passions of men and women.

The Greek word used in the New Testament in reference to the Holy Spirit is *Paraclete.* In the various editions of the New Testament this word is translated "comforter," "advocate," "counselor," and "helper." The word literally means "one who comes and stands beside you to give strength and courage." And the Holy Spirit does just that. He is our counselor in time of decision. He is our helper in time of heavy responsibility. He is our defender in time of temptation. He is our comforter in the time of sorrow and disappointment.

Five prepositions are helpful in understanding the ministry of the Holy Spirit. The first word I would lift up is *with* (John

14:17). This reminds us of the omnipresence of God. He is closer than hands or feet, even the air we breathe. Have you ever said, "God is here today"? The truth is that God is always present. Sometimes he reveals himself more than at other times and there are occasions when we are more sensitive to his presence. He is with all men and women.

Jesus said, "he . . . will be *in* you" (John 14:17).

The Holy Spirit is with all persons but he is uniquely present *in* the life of a believer. "Don't you know that you yourselves are God's temple and that God's Spirit lives in you?" (1 Corinthians 3:16).

Becoming a Christian is more than joining the church, being baptized, and living a decent life. It is being born of the Spirit (John 3:3). "[N]o one can say, 'Jesus is Lord,' except by the Holy Spirit" (1 Corinthians 12:3).

The third preposition is *on.* The last word of Jesus before his ascension was, "you will receive power when the Holy Spirit comes *on* you" (Acts 1:8). In the New Testament there are Christians and then there are Spirit-filled believers. All Christians have received the Holy Spirit but all have not been filled with the Spirit. The Lord usually chooses to use the Spirit-filled believer.

The next preposition I would call your attention to is *out.* In speaking of the Holy Spirit, in John 7:38 Jesus says, "'Whoever believes in me, as the Scripture has said, streams of living water will flow from within [*out of*] him.' By this he meant the Spirit, whom those who believed in him were later to receive." As we become a channel of the Holy Spirit our lives become fruitful. The Holy Spirit is not just for our enjoyment and blessing but, rather, he equips us and enables us to be a blessing to others. We become a conduit through whom the Spirit flows.

The last preposition that I would suggest to you is *by.* It is by the power of the Holy Spirit that we shall have a personal resurrection (Romans 8:11).

The Holy Spirit Is Power

Power was evident in the primitive church because it was a Spirit-filled church. "With great power the apostles continued to testify to the resurrection of the Lord Jesus" (Acts 4:33). This *power* is available for us. The power is of the Holy Spirit. The power *is* the Holy Spirit. When we receive him we receive power. Before he ascended into heaven, Jesus said to his disciples, "stay in the city [Jerusalem] until you have been clothed with power from on high" (Luke 24:49).

The power given to the disciples is energy. All who are baptized with the Spirit have divine energy, power, strength. Who are the Spirit-filled Christians? The answer is in the word *witness*. This word in the New Testament Greek has the same root as the word *martyr*. A martyr is a person who dies for a cause. When one dies to sin and self, trusts Jesus Christ, and claims the promise of the Father, that person is filled with the Holy Spirit.

He Is the Divine Prompter

He is the Divine Prompter or Persuader. "But the Counselor, the Holy Spirit, whom the Father will send in my name, will teach you all things and will remind you of everything I have said to you" (John 14:26). Were you ever in a school play and forgot your lines and there was a prompter behind the curtain to remind you? That is what the Holy Spirit does—he reminds us.

"[N]o one can say, 'Jesus is Lord,' except by the Holy Spirit" (1 Corinthians 12:3). The Holy Spirit leads us to Jesus. He always honors Christ. He does not call attention to himself but to Jesus. Any experience or gift that distracts from Jesus is not of the Holy Spirit. It is not authentic.

As the Persuader he convinces, convicts and reproves. "When he comes, he will convict the world of guilt in regard to sin and righteousness and judgment" (John 16:8). We fail to win people because we rely upon human ability rather than Spirit-anointed persuasion. Persons must be convicted of their lost condition. This is the work of the Holy Spirit. Individuals must be convinced of their need of Christ. This is the ministry of the Holy Spirit. Much of our evangelism fails because it is in the energy of the flesh rather than in the power of the Spirit.

As the Prompter he will guide the Christian to truth. "But when he, the Spirit of truth, comes, he will guide you into all truth . . . He will bring glory to me" (John 16:13–14). The Holy Spirit is our teacher. We are not left to make our decisions alone. He will guide. He will never lead you contrary to his Word but will speak to us through his Word. He will never lead you away from the spirit, teachings and person of Jesus Christ. He is not the message but points men and women to the message—Jesus Christ. He is not the central personality but always makes Jesus central. He does not speak of himself but leads men and women to speak of Jesus. He is not an end, but rather, a means to the Alpha and Omega, the First and the Last, Jesus Christ.

He Is the Purifier

He is the Purifier. He imparts sanctifying grace to the heart of the believer. He fulfills the prayer of Paul: "May God himself, the God of peace, sanctify you through and through. May your whole spirit, soul and body be kept blameless at the coming of the Lord Jesus Christ" (1 Thessalonians 5:23).

Romans 5:5 declares, "God has poured out his love into our hearts by the Holy Spirit, whom he has given us." And read these Scriptures: "[F]rom the beginning God chose you to be saved through the sanctifying work of the Spirit and through belief in the truth" (2 Thessalonians 2:13); "God, who knows the heart, showed that he accepted them by giving the Holy Spirit to them, just as did to us. He made no distinction between us and them, for he purified their hearts by faith" (Acts 15:8–9).

Notes

1   Andrew Blackwood, Jr., *The Holy Spirit in Your Life* (Grand Rapids: Baker Book House, 1957), pp. 147–150.

2   Edmund W. Robb, Jr., *The Person and Ministry of The Holy Spirit,* (Abilene, Texas: Evangelical Publishers, 1971), pp. 23–27.

CHAPTER 5

Life in the Spirit

The 'Fruit' That Makes Christian Living Sweet

*I*n the nineteenth chapter of the Acts, the Apostle Paul is recorded as preaching to the church at Ephesus. He asked this question, "Did you receive the Holy Spirit when you believed?" They answered, "No, we have not even heard that there is a Holy Spirit" (Acts 19:2).

The ignorance Christians often display concerning the Holy Spirit continues to shock me. However, I think I understand why so many people are turned off by talk of the Spirit. They have seen people who talk a lot about the Holy Spirit. Those "Spirit-filled" types have seemed strange to them, and people don't want to be strange and odd. But if you are strange the Holy Spirit didn't make you that way. You were strange before you ever heard of the Holy Spirit. The Holy Spirit should bring balance and wholeness to persons.

More Christians would begin to open themselves up to the ministry of the Holy Spirit if they understood that the Spirit is not *primarily* about miracles and gifts. Rather, the Spirit gives us the power to *internalize* the faith, to be Christians from the inside out.

When we are living the Spirit-filled life, we are finally able to do the things we know we ought to do and live the way we ought to live. We have peace and joy, and all those other wonderful traits Paul called the "fruit of the Spirit." Some people may have their doubts about gifts, but everyone ought to welcome the fruit.

The Plague of Legalism

Conservative Christianity has too often been cursed with the plague of legalism. Many unhappy believers stagger through life in the bondage of rules, "dos and don'ts," superimposed cultural expectations, and fear. Negative religion is not very attractive. I have known sincere Christians who have never experienced the joy of their salvation. They are on a continuous guilt trip because they never quite measure up to their expectations. These defeated believers have never claimed the glorious liberty of being the children of God.

Why do many Christians live in fear of judgment rather than feeling fired up for Jesus Christ? Unfortunately, too many are simply thinking as they have been taught to think. Many pastors continually preach commitment but do not proclaim the grace that enables one to be committed and victorious. Their churches are filled with defeated persons who need the liberating power of the Spirit.

A year or two after my father became a Christian he quit smoking. He became so irritable he made everyone miserable. My mother hated cigarettes but she was relieved when he went back to smoking after one month. Two years later, in a great revival, my father had a wonderful Christian experience. He quit smoking and never touched another cigarette. The desire for tobacco was taken away. He didn't quit in his own strength but out of an encounter with the Holy Spirit.

Obviously, not everyone will experience a miraculous deliverance from addiction, but it is true that the grace and love of God is a far better motivator than guilt. When my dad felt the joy of his salvation (a fruit of the Spirit) coursing through him, he had the strength he needed to quit. The positive overcame the negative.

The Folly of Man-made Religion

I have a friend who as a new Christian went to a denominational retreat. The speakers were burdened because of the injustices of the world. Famines, wars, poverty and natural disasters concerned them. However there was no word about personal forgiveness and grace. It was my friend's impression that defeated women and men were challenging defeated persons to reform the world.

Later, my friend attended an evangelical retreat. There was praise and rejoicing. Persons were testifying to their salvation in Jesus Christ. This crowd went out to witness and serve in the power of the Spirit.

The institutionalists were challenging people to serve out of duty. The evangelicals were excited to serve the Lord out of the overflow of their experience. How much more attractive and effective this approach is.

Occasionally in the past I have become ultra-religious. Determined to make myself saintly, I would announce that I was going to follow a simple lifestyle, get up at five each morning to pray for two hours and follow the spiritual disciplines of a consecrated life. There was nothing wrong with my desire to be more dedicated. The problem was that I was seeking to do this in my own strength rather than in response to a vital experience with the Lord. It was legalism rather than grace. Martha would dread these times because I only succeeded in making everyone miserable, including myself. When these disciplines come out of a walk with the Lord, however, it is different.

A Better Way to Follow God

If duty is not the way we become strong enough to follow God's will, then how do we? The New Testament teaches that our personal relationship with Christ—through the Holy Spirit—helps us overcome all stumbling blocks.

Paul captures this new way of looking at right versus wrong when he writes to the church in Corinth in his second letter. I'm quoting from the third chapter from *The Message,* a brilliant translation by Eugene Peterson:

> Whenever, though, they [the children of Israel] turn to face God as Moses did, God removes the veil and there they are—face to face! They suddenly recognize that God is a living, personal presence, not a piece of chiseled stone [the commandments]. And when God is personally present, a living Spirit, that old, constricting legislation is recognized as obsolete. We're free of it! All of us! Nothing between us and God, our faces shining with the brightness of his face. And so we are transfigured much like the Messiah, our lives gradually becoming brighter and more beautiful as God enters our lives and we become like him.[1]

In other words, we are given the fruit of self-control naturally as our attention is fixed on Christ. We don't have to subdue our natures through brute force. Our love of him gives us the will and the strength to obey.

The Path to Disaster

Many are caught in a spiritual trap. They are sincere in their faith but unfulfilled. Some are saying the right things but have not experienced the reality in their lives. Some are playing a game that they are going to lose. They know the steps but they can't hear the music.

This is the path to disaster or disillusionment. It sometimes leads to an inability to cope with the pressures of life and results in a kind of stoicism or cynical resignation. In other words, since they have not yet experienced God's fullness, they tend to knock down those who have. They take on the smug, knowing looks of secular unbelievers. These attitudes are a kind of surrender, and they will lead to total spiritual burnout.

I was a shoe salesman while working my way through college. Occasionally in the zeal of my youth I would witness to the customers. The store manager became irritated with me and said, "Ed, you are on fire now, but just wait until you are past 40, those old dead church members will take it all out of you." I still remember my 40th birthday. I was tempted to call my former boss and say, "Bill, I'm 40 but I am still on fire for Jesus Christ."

But I now know what he was talking about. Youth has a natural exuberance, a zest for life. As we get older this tends to fade. If we don't continue a close walk with the Lord, our joy and enthusiasm for life will decline and eventually lead to disillusionment.

Most of us have seen persons like that. They hear of a conversion and they say, "It won't last." I remember as a boy, we had a great revival in my home church. An alcoholic was gloriously converted. Many said, "It won't last," but it did. He never took another drink.

When there are reports of miraculous healings there are those who say, "There must be some other explanation." And sometimes there is—but at other times God has clearly intervened.

I remember when the Lay Witness missions swept across the church. There was great excitement. Many had new and deeper experiences in the Lord. I recall one of the older church members saying, "I've seen the church get excited before. This won't last long." But it did. Thousands were brought into the kingdom and many into the ministry through the Lay Witness missions.

Another danger of cynicism is a surrender to temptation. Many are governed by a feeling of "oughtness," but are in reality spiritually empty. When temptation comes, they are more likely to say, "Why not?"

I have a minister friend who was outstanding. He had a very successful pastorate, with a rapidly growing big-city church. He would work 15–16 hours a day. Obviously, this talented man left little time for his family and his personal life. Victory after victory came to this growing church. At the same time, however, the pastor neglected his devotional life.

Without realizing it, he gradually cut himself off from the Spirit. The all-important fruit of the Spirit was his no longer, including self-control. In a time of carnal temptation he proved vulnerable. He yielded and it ruined a very fruitful ministry. He knew the steps but he had ceased to hear the music.

Is this the normal Christian life? Must we have a divided, rebellious heart? Is there no victory for the Christian? Must the believer have a life of frustration?

A Life of Holiness—the Essence of the Spirit's Fruit

Christians can have a life of holiness rather than defeat. Paul wrote, "You have been set free from sin and have become slaves to righteousness" (Romans 6:18).

Holiness is not a human achievement but rather a gift one receives. Our salvation comes by virtue of the imputed righteousness received by faith in Christ. He is our "righteousness, holiness and redemption" (1 Corinthians 1:30).

As believers we not only have judicial (legal) righteousness because of our faith in Christ but we also experience imparted righteousness. That is, not only does Christ's blood cover us, but he cleanses us and enables us to live a holy (righteous) life. We read in 1 John 1:7, "if we walk in the light, as he is in the light, we have fellowship with one another, and the blood of Jesus, his Son, purifies us from every sin." We are encouraged by the promise, "where sin increased, grace increased all the more" (Romans 5:20).

To boil the whole matter down to a phrase, the essence of the "fruit of the Spirit" *is* holiness. The description of holiness is found in Galatians 5:22: "love, joy, peace, patience, kindness, goodness, faithfulness, gentleness and self control." These are universally respected characteristics. The great word of religion is holiness. Holiness is wholeness, holiness is health, holiness brings balance. Holiness does not concern itself primarily with what we do not do, but rather, what the Spirit enables us to do.

Holiness is not the length of one's sleeves or the color of one's lips but rather the condition of one's heart. For some legalists, holiness is a retreat to nineteenth-century culture. It is characterized with such negatives as, "don't smoke, don't drink, don't chew, and don't go with those that do." This narrowness is a mistake, for the spirit of holiness is contemporary, for every age and culture.

Living a Spirit-filled life must not be equated with renouncing our bodies, including the sex drive. Too many conservative Christians have turned sex into a forbidden topic. For the healthy minded, all of God's creation is good. Sex is not something to be ashamed of and considered dirty. But within the covenant of marriage it is an expression of love and a fulfilling experience. Sex without love will ultimately be destructive. Sex within the marriage relationship in the bond of love can be one of the most rewarding experiences of one's life. This is not contrary to holiness but a blessing of the holy life.

To Be Fully Human

Holiness is not life-denying, but life-affirming. It enables one to become *fully* human. It does not call for one to suppress her

or his humanity but enables one to fully express that humanity.
It gives one a great capacity for life.

Some would picture a sanctified person as pale, anemic, and
puny. Perhaps they believe they are so heavenly minded they are
no earthly good.

My hero in the faith and my father in Christ was Dr. J. C.
McPheeters. He had a great capacity for life. Dr. McPheeters
loved to hunt and fish. He seemed to enjoy life to the fullest. He
learned to water-ski when he was past 70. Every morning he
was up before dawn doing his calisthenics and having his devo-
tions. I never heard him say a negative word about anyone. He
was optimistic and excited about life. Dr. McPheeters was not
wanting to retreat into the past but rather to march boldly into
the future conquering for Christ.

But at age 93 Dr. McPheeters had a stroke and lost his ability to speak. Whenever he would try to communicate he would
say, "I will arise." This was so typical of him—and he did! He
went to be with the Lord at age 94.

Sustained by Discipline

As I have said elsewhere in this book, anything that is meaningful causes deep feeling. To be saved from deep-seated feeling
of guilt certainly should lead to the emotion of praise and thanksgiving.

However, having said that, I want to add that many persons
expect to be on a spiritual high all the time. This is unrealistic.
We go to the mountain to be renewed and empowered that we
may go into the valley where the sins, hurts and needs are, to
serve in the name of Christ. During the dry periods if we walk
in faith and obedience, the feelings of joy and assurance will
return. Dry periods will come. Often it is the result of exhaus-
tion, perhaps sickness, and it may be from an all-out attack by
Satan. Hang on to your faith, observe the spiritual disciplines
and the victory will return.

Spiritual Disciplines Necessary for Spiritual Victory

A vital *prayer life* is necessary to victorious living. Archbishop William Temple, the head of the Anglican communion during World War II, has written, "I notice when I pray the delightful coincidences occur more often." Serendipity! Hasn't this been the experience of most Christians? Truly, nothing lies beyond the power of prayer that is not outside the will of God. An important characteristic of meaningful prayer is praise. Someone has rightly said, "It is impossible to praise God and be depressed at the same time."

Bible reading must not be neglected. Dwight L. Moody, the great nineteenth-century evangelist, has been quoted as saying, "Sin will keep you from the Word, or the Word will keep you from sin." There is a lot of truth in that statement. The Bible inspires our faith, convicts us of our sins, challenges us to serve and witness, and is a means of grace to strengthen us in our Christian walk. The mistake of some Spirit-filled Christians is to rely on experience to the neglect of Scripture study. This can lead to instability. Our faith must be anchored in and disciplined by the written Word of God.

The public *worship* of God is a necessary means of grace. I have noticed many who are enamored of the gifts of the Spirit are weak in their loyalty to the church. They tend to drift to wherever they discern the action is. Their loyalty seems to be to an experience rather than to the body of Christ.

Our loyalty is to Christ, of course, but we need the discipline of worshiping God with the same congregation in the same place regularly. And that congregation needs the witness of Spirit-filled believers who are loyal church persons.

A vital part of worship is the sacrament of *the Lord's Supper.* Many evangelicals do not seem to have a proper appreciation for Holy Communion. The Eucharist is the highest act of worship, I believe. The Scriptures teach consubstantiation; that is, the Lord is objectively present in Holy Communion. We partake of him spiritually in receiving the elements of bread and wine. Where the Lord is uniquely realized, there the Lord uniquely is. He meets us at his table.

Christian fellowship is necessary to a life in the Spirit. Christianity is a social religion. It must be expressed and shared. We are strengthened and inspired by the witness of fellow believers. One cannot have a victorious walk with the Lord alone.

Fresh Anointings of the Spirit

Every believer needs fresh anointings of the Holy Spirit. A onetime experience is not enough. Many testify to being "baptized in the Holy Spirit" but have been relying on an experience that is no longer active. They need fresh outpourings of the Holy Spirit.

All of us need a fresh touch of the Spirit from time to time. This is the reason many churches in the past conducted revival meetings. They knew that experiences needed to be renewed. Today, it is important for committed Christians to attend spiritual-life retreats or convocations. Small group meetings are helpful. We must keep our experience vital and dynamic. Local church revivals can still be effective for renewal.

The church does not need a new program from Nashville. It needs a fresh outpouring of the Holy Spirit from heaven. Too often we have relied on the energy of the flesh rather than the power of the Spirit.

Recently, I went back to Cissna Park, Illinois. Twenty-five years ago, I was there for an area-wide crusade. The services were under a big tent. Much prayer and careful preparation was given by the cooperating churches. The spirit was good from the beginning. Each evening the crowds increased and decisions were made for Christ. It was an eight-day crusade and the last service was Sunday evening. That afternoon there came a terrible thunderstorm. The counseling tent was blown down. The big tent was leaking. Many cars were stuck in the mud. Despite all of this the tent was overflowing with people. When I gave the invitation I was overwhelmed with the response. Scores were saved that night and many others rededicated their lives.

That crusade made a lasting impact on the community. Many have come to me and said, "I was converted 25 years ago in the great crusade"; others have said, "My life was changed when I made a public decision the night God came in the crusade many years ago."

Revivals are still taking place today.

Our walk in the Spirit must not be so mystical that it is not expressed in practical ways. We cannot be blind to the needs of this world. Spirit-filled believers should have compassion on the poor, seek to help the weak, become involved in reform efforts to make this world a better place to live and be involved citizens in their community. Too long we have turned our communities over to the secularists. Part of our Christian witness should be serving the world in the name of Christ.

Every minister admitted into a United Methodist annual conference has been asked the following questions:

1. Have you faith in Christ?
2. Are you going on to perfection?
3. Do you expect to be made perfect in love in this life?
4. Are you earnestly striving after it?

Perfect love should be the goal of every Christian and the result of holiness (1 John 4:12). You may recall, the list of the fruit of the Spirit names *love* first. I once had a bishop who would pause during ordination and ask the candidates, "If you are not going on to perfection, where are you going?"

Life Is a Celebration

Life in the Spirit should be a celebration. The early Methodists were often called "the shouting Methodists" because they were overcome by joy. They were a singing people. The Spirit-filled life was one of spontaneity. The spiritual song, "The Methodist" was so esteemed that it was put in the cornerstones of Foundry Methodist Church in Washington, D.C.

> The *World*, the *Devil*, and *Tom Paine*
> Have try'd their force, but all in vain.
> They can't prevail, the reason is,
> The Lord defends the Methodist.
>
> They pray, they sing, they preach the best,
> And do the Devil most molest.
> If Satan had his vicious way,
> He'd kill and damn them all today.
>
> They are despised by Satan's train,
> Because they shout and preach so plain.
> I'm bound to march in endless bliss,
> And die a shouting Methodist.

The United Methodist Hymnal contains a hymn written by Samuel Longfellow in 1864 that is a moving request to be filled with the Holy Spirit. More than a century later, it is still a worthy prayer.

> Holy Spirit, Truth divine,
> dawn upon this soul of mine;
> Word of God and inward light,
> wake my spirit, clear my sight.
>
> Holy Spirit, Love divine,
> glow within this heart of mine;
> kindle every high desire;
> perish self in thy pure fire.
>
> Holy Spirit, Power divine,
> fill and nerve this will of mine;

grant that I may strongly live,
bravely bear, and nobly strive.

Holy Spirit, Right divine,
King within my conscience reign;
be my Lord, and I shall be
firmly bound, forever free.

Notes

1 Eugene Peterson, *The Message: the New Testament in Contemporary English* (Colorado Springs: NavPress, 1993), p. 373.

CHAPTER 6

The Spirit Who Will Not Be Tamed

Lessons from Wesley's Revival and the Second Great Awakening

*N*early 70 years ago E. Stanley Jones said, "One of the greatest needs of our day, if not the greatest need, is a rediscovery of the Holy Spirit."[1] His assessment was correct then, and it's still right today.

Unfortunately, believers of different stripes are at odds over how to experience the Spirit in a healthful, balanced way. Traditionalists have emphasized the fruit of the Spirit (Galatians 5:22–23), while often neglecting the gifts. Charismatics and Pentecostals, on the other hand, have primarily concerned themselves with the gifts of the Spirit (1 Corinthians 12:7–11, 28–31; Romans 12:6–8; Ephesians 4:11–12), sometimes giving little emphasis to the fruit.

We need both. We can learn from each other. The church needs the freedom, contemporary expression, excitement, and zeal of the Charismatics. But we also need the ethical emphasis, discipline, theological depth, and churchmanship of the Wesleyan traditionalists.

A church without the ongoing empowerment of the Holy Spirit soon tires, grows moldy, shrinks and eventually dies. If you do not believe that, look all around you. Stanley Jones was right—the Spirit is not a luxury that only extra-spiritual Christians need bother with. He is God within us!

The good news is that the Holy Spirit *is* being rediscovered today, as he has by various groups for 2,000 years.

A Tradition of Ignoring the Gifts

I once thought that the "gifts" ceased to be operative with the completion of the New Testament canon at the end of the Apostolic age. This conviction was the result of prejudice and wrong-headed teaching (more on that later). Only as I matured did I discover that the Holy Spirit was bigger than my parochial view of him. The work of the Spirit is not always neat, and it took me many years to understand that.

The history of the church shows that the Holy Spirit has been ignored or played down as a rule.

During the Protestant Reformation, the Lutheran and Reformed theologians seldom mentioned the spiritual gifts. When Luther discussed spiritual gifts, he identified them with talents or material blessings. Calvin espoused the point of view that the supernatural gifts of the Holy Spirit ceased with the death of the last apostle.

Many Protestants of past generations have followed John Calvin in regarding spiritual gifts as temporary manifestations experienced only in the days of the apostles. Reformed theologian Benjamin B. Warfield wrote in *Counterfeit Miracles*, ". . . the extraordinary gifts belonged to the extraordinary office [apostleship] and showed themselves only in connection with its activities."[2]

Likewise, the Church of England during Wesley's day rarely made reference to the Spirit outside of its Sunday services and its *Book of Common Prayer*. The Anglicans insisted that religious expression remain strictly bounded by tradition. If believers exhibited the fruit of the spirit, such as love, that was well and good. But Anglican authorities had little use for the gifts of the Spirit. Indeed, religious "enthusiasm" was seen as tasteless at best.

John Wesley, however, proved an enormous exception to this closed-mindedness. If John Wesley were living today, I believe he would affirm the Charismatic movement. In his early career, as noted in earlier chapters, Wesley was hyper-conservative in his style. But after Aldersgate, he began opening his mind to new concepts. Gifts of the Holy Spirit deeply interested him.

An Early Pentecostal Movement

Wesley looked back to the teachings of Montanus, a second-century revivalist and, possibly, a prophet. Montanus was something like an early Pentecostal, claiming to speak directly for God from a trance-like state. He and his followers emphasized the immediate working of the Holy Spirit. Although pure in intention, they erred in insisting on an excessive supernaturalism and a radical puritanism (i.e., if you fall from grace, you cannot recover). Within several decades the church rejected Montanism. But in doing so, church leaders overreacted. They preferred order to what they regarded as the chaos of Montanism.

The church made clear how it should *not* be done. But it was vague at best on how Christians *could* express the Holy Spirit and the gifts. This resulted in spiritual gifts being almost completely neglected.

I quote from Wesley's journal concerning the Montanists:

> By reflecting on an odd book which I read in this journey, "The General Delusion of Christians with regard to Prophecy," I was fully convinced of what I had long suspected, 1. That the Montanists, in the second and third centuries, were real, scriptural Christians; and, 2. That the grand

reason why the miraculous gifts were so soon withdrawn, was not only that faith and holiness were well nigh lost; but that dry, formal, orthodox men began even then to ridicule whatever gifts they had not themselves, and to decry them as either madness or imposture.[3]

Could not these same attitudes be the source of much of the opposition to the Charismatic movement today?

Pentecostal-Style Happenings in the Wesleyan Revival

Earlier we discussed how John Wesley began teaching about the new birth and sanctification of the Holy Spirit. His preaching of these novel doctrines led to what we now call "the Wesleyan Revival." Wesley took the revolutionary step of preaching out-of-doors, going where the common people were. Crowds sometimes numbering in the tens of thousands came to hear him preach the need for repentance and the new birth.

Thousands were converted, and many did not come along quietly. There was loud weeping and shouting from grief-stricken sinners. Under Wesley's preaching persons would have the "jerks" or "shakes" or they might be what is called today "slain in the spirit." Others experienced prophetic dreams during Wesley's visits and afterwards. Though Wesley apparently never participated directly by expressing religious ecstasy, neither did he discourage it. I recently read in Wesley's journal:

> Our Lord was present in an uncommon manner. Some dropped down as dead; but, after a while, rejoiced with joy unspeakable. One was carried away in violent fits. I went to her after the service. She was strongly convulsed from head to foot, and shrieked out in a dreadful manner. The unclean spirit did tear her indeed; but his reign was not long. In the morning both her soul and body were healed and she acknowledged both the justice and mercy of God.

George Whitefield, Wesley's fellow evangelist, became concerned about these unusual manifestations and wrote John Wesley a critical letter:

> I cannot think it right in you to give so much encouragement to those convulsions which people have been thrown into, under your ministry. Was I to do so, how many would cry out every night? I think it is tempting God to require such signs. That there is something of God in it, I doubt not. But the devil, I believe, does interpose. I think it will encourage the French Prophets [a heretical group emphasizing the Holy Spirit], take people from the written word, and make them depend on visions, convulsions, &c., more than on the promises and precepts of the Gospels. Honored Sir, how could you tell that some who came to "were in a good measure sanctified." What fruits could be produced in one night's time?[4]

But in this Whitefield underestimated Wesley, who was hardly a sentimentalist. Wesley did not judge quickly or by outside appearances. During the early days of the revival Wesley described how he cast out a violent demon. He wrote that his test for judging such a spiritual experience was that:

> . . . such a change was then wrought appears (not from their shedding tears only, or falling into fits, or crying out: These are not the fruits, . . . whereby I judge, but) from the whole tenor of these life, till then, [was in] many ways wicked; from that time, holy, just, and good.[5]

Whitefield's criticisms of Pentecostal occurrences sound remarkably similar to the things non-Charismatic evangelicals say about Charismatics and Pentecostals, don't they?

Later, however, Whitefield recorded that similar incidents were occurring in his ministry. In light of his earlier criticism of Wesley, it seems obvious Whitefield was doing nothing to stir up emotionalism. However, his writing shows that he began to view these experiences much more positively:

> A wonderful Power was in the Room, and with one Accord they began to cry out and weep most bitterly for the Space of half an Hour. They seemed to be under the strongest Convictions . . . Their Cries might be heard a great Way off . . . five of them seemed affected as those that are in Fits . . . and at midnight I was desired to come to one who was in strong Agonies.
>
> Look where I would, most were drowned in Tears. The Word was sharper than a two-edged Sword, and their bitter Cries and Groans were enough to pierce the hardest Heart. Oh what different Visages were then to be seen? Some were struck pale as Death, others wringing their hands, others lying on the Ground, others sinking into the Arms of their Friends, and most lifting up their Eyes toward Heaven, and crying out to God. I could think of nothing, when I looked at them, so much as the Great Day—They seemed like Persons awakened by the last Trump.[6]

The Revival Moves on to America

Although Methodism had at first enjoyed rapid growth in America, by the beginning of the nineteenth century it had peaked. The eastern U.S. was stained by the heresies of deism and universalism (all will be saved). The frontier states of Kentucky and Tennessee were mostly outright pagan and very wild. But the frontier is exactly where the Second Great Awakening broke out.

Prayer came first. In 1798 the Presbyterian General Assembly set aside a day for fasting and repentance. Local churches began enforcing church discipline, and members began praying for revival. In the year 1800 things began to break loose. At the

Red River Presbyterian Church, in central Kentucky, a revival began during the annual communion. As a minister preached, several people began loudly weeping, searching for the assurance of their salvation. One woman in particular cried out, and a Methodist preacher attending the event went to comfort her. On the way to her side, he was warned that this was a Presbyterian church, where no emotionalism would be allowed.

However, the minister, John McGee wrote:

I turned to go back and was near falling; the power of God was strong upon me. I turned again and, losing sight of the fear of man, I went through the house shouting exhorting with all possible ecstasy and energy, and the floor was soon covered with the slain.[7]

The lid had blown off, so to speak, and it wasn't going to be put back on. Word of this outbreak spread fast. In August, 1801, at a site near Cane Ridge Presbyterian Church, near Lexington, Kentucky, a gigantic encampment of about 20,000 seekers met for another communion, hoping for a repeat of the previous year. And the Spirit of God fell with extraordinary power. What resulted was "arguably... the most important religious gathering in all of American history."[8]

In a day before rural restaurants, portable toilets, or motels, getting a crowd of this size together for days at a time in itself showed an amazing dedication. Their sacrifices did not go unrewarded.

It is estimated that between 1,000 and 3,000 persons were saved during this first camp meeting, and many more repented of their sins loudly. The emotional preaching whipped up a great deal of anxiety, and perhaps this explains some of what happened at Cane Ridge and later meetings.

In the early camp meetings in America shouting the praises of God was not unusual. Ben Witherington, in an article written for *Challenge to Evangelism Today*, records, "There would be swooning that led into a coma-like state sometimes for minutes or even for hours. Often this was described using familiar military metaphors—the preacher fired a shot into Satan's ranks and many were moved and fell. People lay around in vast numbers like corpses, and were often dragged off to a remote spot, but still the service went on."[9]

But the Cane Ridge revival also saw more gentle spiritual manifestations. Journalist Mark Galli reports:

> Almost anyone—women, small children, slaves, the shy, the illiterate—could exhort with great effect.
>
> One 7-year-old girl mounted a man's shoulders and spoke wondrous words until she was completely fatigued. When she lay her head on his as if to sleep, someone in the audience suggested "the poor thing" had better be laid down to rest. The girl roused and said, "Don't call me poor, for Christ is my brother, God my father, and I have a kingdom to inherit, and therefore do not call me poor, for I am rich in the blood of the lamb!"[10]

James Fenley reports he had once gone to gawk at a camp meeting. He heard 1,000 shout at once as if shot—he said he saw what appeared to be a vast sea of humans swaying back and forth as if agitated by a storm. Soon he began to realize that a huge supernatural force had hold of them. His heart began to beat rapidly and his knees got weak, and his lips quivered. Fenley realized he was about to be overcome and fled into the woods, drank a bit and spent a miserable night on a haystack. On the way home he wept over his misspent life, repenting of his sins. At dawn the next day he went into the woods to pray, was converted and later got the call to preach.

The Reality Behind the Experiences

After reading the above passages, it is natural to wonder how many of these happenings were actually directed by the

Holy Spirit, and how many were the result of mass hysteria, autosuggestion, and the like. What is the reality?

I believe the Spirit *does* work through these unusual, excitable outpourings. Yet I also recognize that there is a human psychological element at work as well. One thing is obvious—these sorts of things generally happen where they are expected and *only* there. In Pentecostal churches people almost *always* speak in tongues, but in non-Pentecostal, non-Charismatic congregations tongues are rarely if ever heard.

Scholar Clarke Garrett analyzes the emotional phenomena of the Wesleyan revival this way:

> There was a subtle dynamic at work between preacher and audience. Whitefield's effectiveness lay to a degree in the fact that he was consciously a performer, utilizing gestures and the modulation of his voice to elicit the intended emotional responses from his audience. Wesley was not at all a performer in that sense, but by some theatrical chemistry he suggested to some of his hearers that they might be acted upon by supernatural power in publicly evoking the private drama of conversion.[11]

One minister charged that Wesley signaled his hearers that such outcries were welcome or even expected by praying aloud "that God would visibly manifest some Token of his Favour."

No doubt there is truth to this. No scholar I have read, including Garrett, believes Wesley was *consciously* manipulating his congregations. His movement did, however, provide a climate friendly to emotional religion, and that's what they got.

Could it be that God works with us within our own theology and psychological makeup? Perhaps a stern, unemotional faith is ideal for one and deadly for another. Some things we will not know this side of heaven.

However, it does seem clear that permanent, dramatic changes in character and lifestyle often follow emotional religious experiences like those described above. Could it be that we humans have a need to humble ourselves visibly and audibly before God and our fellow worshipers for real change to take place?

Supernatural Healings

Accounts of excitement during revival services are interesting, but as I've noted they are not conclusive. Does anything more lasting come from these experiences of the Holy Spirit? Healing of the body should be considered.

The Charismatics today teach and practice supernatural healing. Perhaps they have overemphasized this aspect of the gospel and sometimes have made claims that cannot be substantiated, but who can deny the clear teaching of Scripture concerning divine healing?

I would remind you of the story of Hezekiah in 2 Kings 20 where the Lord healed the king and gave him 15 more years of life. The Psalmist affirms healing with these words, "He . . . heals all my diseases" (Psalm 103:3). The New Testament is full of healing experiences such as the story of the lame man begging at the temple gate called Beautiful. Peter said, "Silver or gold I do not have, but what I have I give you. In the name of Jesus Christ of Nazareth, walk" (Acts 3:6).

Some would argue that supernatural healing was limited to the apostolic age but the promise in the book of James does not seem to be limited to any period. "Is any one of you sick? He should call the elders of the church to pray over him and anoint him with oil in the name of the Lord. And the prayer offered in faith will make the sick person well; the Lord will raise him up" (James 5:14–15).

In reading Wesley's journals I find many instances of miraculous healings:

> The Physician told me he could do no more; Mr. Myrick could not live over the night. I went up, and found them

all crying around him, his legs being cold, and (as it seemed) dead already. We all kneeled down, and called upon God with strong cries and tears. He opened his eyes, and called for me; and, from that hour, he continued to recover his strength, till he was restored to perfect health. I wait to hear who will either disprove this fact, or philosophically account for it.[12]

In reporting another healing Wesley shows an astounding early understanding of the psychological aspects of medicine. He stated:

Reflecting to-day on the case of a poor woman who had continual pain in her stomach, I could not but remark the inexcusable negligence of most Physicians in cases of this nature. They prescribe drug upon drug, without knowing a jot of the matter concerning the root of the disorder. And without knowing this, they cannot cure, though they can murder, the patient. Whence came this woman's pain? (which she would never have told, had she never been questioned about it): From fretting for the death of her son. And what availed medicines, while that fretting continued? Why then do not all Physicians consider how far bodily disorders are caused or influenced by the mind; and in those cases, which are utterly out of their sphere, call in the assistance of a Minister; as Ministers, when they find the mind disordered by the body, call in the assistance of a Physician? But why are these cases out of their sphere? Because they know not God. It follows, no man can be a thorough Physician without being an experienced Christian.[13]

. . . My teeth pained me much. In coming home, Mr. Spear gave me an account of the rupture he had for some years, which, after the most eminent Physicians had declared it incurable, was perfectly cured in a moment. I prayed with submission to the will of God. My pain ceased, and returned no more.[14]

Authentic Spiritual Movements Bring Character Change

Ultimately, neither emotional outpouring nor even spiritual healings can authenticate a spiritual movement. For modern outpourings like the Pentecostal and Charismatic movements, the real test is whether they form an improved human character. The Wesleyan revival passed this test. Let's examine it in that light.

Evangelism

They taught the necessity of personal experience. Surely, they would have agreed with General William Booth, founder of the Salvation Army, when he said, "Religion is like a cup of tea, it is no good unless it is hot."

Evangelism was their highest priority and they witnessed transformed lives. In a brief research of the Wesleyan revival I find these testimonies:

- One woman responding to criticism of Mr. Wesley said, "One thing I know, he changed liquor into furniture for me." Her husband had been converted.
- A husband testifies that the Methodists have silenced his wife's "scolding tongue."
- A soldier on the way to a prostitute was invited to a Methodist watch night service, from which he walks away rejoicing in the straight and narrow life.
- A barber, who was the most imminent of drunkards, is made sober.
- A poor despairing soul is diverted from suicide.

My question is, "Where are the converts of Wesleyan Christians today?" Has the gospel lost its power to save?

Bishop Francis Ensley has written, "A preacher of religion who can promise deliverance from alcohol, cigarettes, gossip, temper, insecurity, domestic failure, guilt, irrational fears and life's emptiness and can persuade humanity of it, *and make good on the promise*—that preacher has the world in his hip pocket." [15]

If we are faithful to the Wesleyan tradition, we will have a message of transforming and sanctifying power and we will see these kinds of results.

Lay Leadership

The Charismatic renewal is primarily a lay-led movement. Many ministers are threatened by zealous lay persons who may have a more intimate relationship to the Lord than they do. Also, Spirit-filled laymen are usually not as institutionally loyal nor submissive. Their theology, especially on the authority of the Scriptures, is likely to be more conservative.

Ministers have a vested interest in the status quo. The "system" is their security blanket. Laymen are more likely to be free in Christ and obedient to the Holy Spirit.

Wesley wrote concerning the great evangelical revival:

". . . He hath not dealt so with any nation;" no, not even with Scotland or New-England. In both these God has indeed made bare his arm; yet not in so astonishing a manner as among us. This must appear to all who impartially consider, 1. The numbers of persons on whom God has wrought; 2. The swiftness of his work in many, both convinced and truly converted in a few days; 3. The depth of it in most of these, changing the heart, as well as the whole conversation; 4. the clearness of it, enabling them boldly to say, "Thou hast loved me; thou hast given thyself for me"; 5. The continuance of it.

God has wrought in Scotland and New-England, at several times, for some weeks or months together; but among us, he has wrought for near eighteen years together, without any observable intermission. Above all, let it be remarked, that a considerable number of the regular Clergy were engaged in that great work in Scotland; and in New-England, above an hundred, perhaps as eminent as any in the whole province, not only for piety, but also for abilities, both natural and acquired; whereas in England there were only two or three inconsiderable Clergymen, with a few young, raw, unlettered men; and these opposed by well nigh all the Clergy, as well as laity, in the nation. He that remarks this must needs own, both that this is a work of God, and that he hath not wrought so in any other nation.[16]

The Wesleyan revival was a lay movement. If we experience a revival in our time it will probably come through lay persons.

Love of Education

Wesleyan Christians pioneered the way in establishing schools and institutions of higher learning. Wherever the church has gone education has followed. Methodists have established more private schools than any institution in America. In fact some have accused us of worshiping at the altar of secular education. However, we have often emphasized the wrong things in that education. The following words of Wesley might be appropriate today:

Our Church requires that Clergymen should be men of learning, and, to this end, have an University education. But many have an University education, and yet no learning at all. Yet these men are ordained! Meantime, one of eminent learning, as well as unblamable behaviour, cannot be ordained *because he was not at the University!* What a mere farce is this! Who would believe that any Christian Bishop would stoop to so poor an evasion?[17]

Couldn't this statement of Wesley be made of the contemporary church?

Lack of Fear

John Wesley was so controversial that the rector of Epworth, his father's old church, refused to let him preach from his pulpit. So Wesley stood on his father's tombstone and preached the unsearchable riches of Jesus Christ. The bishop of London rebuked him for preaching in his diocese without permission. Wesley replied, "The world is my parish." Wesley was not bound by the conventions of his day.

Alonzo Dow is an excellent example of the "controversial" preacher in early American Methodism. Dow was crossing a river in a ferry. The ferry-boat captain was a notorious sinner with a reputation for violence. The captain did not recognize Dow. He hated Methodists and he said that if he ever met that preacher Alonzo Dow, he would beat him half to death. Dow stood up and said, "Sir, I am Alonzo Dow and I am going to baptize you in the name of the devil whom you serve continually." And according to Bishop Paul Martin in his Dennison Lectures series, Dow threw the ferry captain into the river. It is said that a Methodist Church stands today on the bank of that river established by the man who was baptized in the name of the devil.[18]

Peter Cartwright, a pioneer Methodist preacher, was preaching at the Annual Conference. The church was packed with people standing in the aisles. Just before he was to preach someone whispered in his ear, "General Andrew Jackson just walked in." Peter Cartwright stood in the pulpit and said, "I understand General Jackson is here. General, if you don't repent you are going to hell just like any other person." It is said the men became great friends because General Jackson admired a man of such boldness.

Do either the Charismatics or the traditionalists meet these standards today? Let us pray that such boldness from the Holy Spirit descend upon us once more!

Notes

1 E. Stanley Jones, "Authentic Proofs of the Spirit," untraced.

2 Benjamin B. Warfield, *Counterfeit Miracles* (New York: Charles Scribner's Sons, 1918), p. 23.

3 *Works, Journal,* Aug. 15, 1750, II:204.

4 Stuart C. Henry, *George Whitefield: Wayfaring Witness* (Nashville: Abingdon Press, 1957), p. 64.

5 *Works, Journal,* May 20, 1739, I:195.

6 This quotation is not traced.

7 Cited in "Revival At Cane Ridge," by Mark Galli, *Christian History,* Issue 45, p. 9.

8 Ibid, p. 11.

9 *Challenge to Evangelism Today,* Fall 1991, Vol. 24, No. 3.

10 Galli, p. 14.

11 Clarke Garrett, *Spirit Possession and Popular Religion* (Baltimore: The Johns Hopkins Press, 1987), p. 82.

12 *Works, Journal,* Dec. 25, 1742, I:406.

13 Ibid., May 12, 1759, II:479

14 Wesley's *Journal* contains many similar accounts. This one cannot be traced.

15 Francis Gerald Ensley, *John Wesley Evangelist* (Nashville: Discipleship Resources, reprinted 1979), p. 19.

16 *Works, Journal,* June 16, 1755, II:335.

17 Ibid, p. 531.

18 Dennison Lectures, Bishop Paul Martin, 1955, Lubbock, Texas.

CHAPTER 7

Holiness Reformers, Pentecostal Pyrotechnics, and Airport Laughter

A Hundred Years of Holy Spirit Movements

*A*ll revivals seem to begin in a great burst of spiritual energy, then become institutionalized, and finally die out. Whatever happened to the Second Great Awakening in America?

It did not die quickly. For most of the first half of the nineteenth century, America's churches were seized with a religious fervor that changed the country forever. The Methodists spread their message of being born again to every corner, and by the year 1850 one third of all Protestants in America were Methodists. Baptists and Presbyterians weren't far behind.

Wherever these churches spread, education, sobriety, and responsible citizenship ventured as well. The Second Great Awakening gave America the evangelical religious culture which dominates to this day. Dead religion keeps trying to assert itself, but something in our collective memory reminds us that God is to be experienced and not just studied.

A Cooling of Spiritual Fervor

By the middle of the 1800s, ministers were beginning to receive formal theological training. And as a result, more formal worship was becoming the norm. The uninhibited revivalism of the earlier camp-meeting period was very gradually being replaced by more respectable religion. Slowly, slowly, the fervor of America's Christian churches began to cool. It wasn't so much a matter of a change in theology—yet—as it was a loss of momentum and power.

Although Methodism continued to grow rapidly (we did not peak out numerically until 1968), the *rate of growth* started to slow. America's Protestants were still overwhelmingly evangelical during the second half of the nineteenth century, but some denominational leaders were beginning to examine the new liberal theology recently imported from Europe.

Rise of the Holiness Movement

Into this gap stepped the Methodist Holiness Movement and other mid-century Holy Spirit theologies. The Holiness Movement started, of all places, in New York City. Mrs. Phoebe Palmer was a Bible teacher who started "Tuesday Meetings" in New York in 1837. The doctrine taught in these meetings emphasized a second work of grace subsequent to salvation—their version of Wesley's "sanctification" experience. By the turn of the twentieth century this experience came to be popularly called "the Baptism of the Holy Spirit."[1] The Holiness proponents often called it the "second blessing."

To receive the second blessing, believers had to surrender everything in their hearts and lives to God. In turn, by faith, the Holy Spirit would purify their hearts and enable them to live a sinless life. This was a more ambitious claim than Wesley had made for his sanctification doctrine. Wesley had made it clear that he meant only *perfection of intent or desire.* Although Wesley felt some might not sin again on earth, he did not expect this to be the norm. In the new Methodist Holiness tradition, however, a sinless life was described as not only possible, but expected.*

The ethical implications of this doctrine were vast. To avoid all sin, adherents had to take special pains to separate from the world. Naturally things like alcohol and tobacco were taboo. Moreover, going to plays (later movies), playing even non-gambling card games, and dancing even in ways as family-oriented as square dancing were not allowed.

The Methodists weren't the only teachers of Holiness. The famous evangelist Charles Finney was from the Reformed tradition (Calvin, Luther, etc.). Yet as he reexamined his theology, he decided that Wesley was right—sin was a personal choice, rather than something over which we have no control. He decided that the only way to beat sin was for the Spirit to overwhelm the Christian's will and drive out the desire to sin. He therefore taught that "entire sanctification is attainable in this life."[2]

The very popular Keswick Movement was another non-Methodist Holiness tradition. It stressed a complete yielding to God and the enthronement of the Holy Spirit in one's heart. Even the evangelistic leader D. L. Moody, usually thought of as a fundamentalist, was heavily influenced by the Holiness tradition, and he had an extremely powerful infilling himself. Although he, like many others I could mention, reinterpreted the Holiness doctrine to fit within his own tradition, he essentially taught a version of Wesley's "sanctification." He urged his students, "Get full of the Holy Spirit."[3]

The worship style preferred by the Holiness movement was often meditative and sweet. The great hymn writer Fanny Crosby turned out hundreds of popular Holiness-oriented texts like, "Perfect submission, all is at rest; / I in my Savior am happy and

---

* It is important to note that as the twentieth century unfolded many Holiness bodies gravitated to the more traditional Wesleyan view of sanctification. That is, though the Holy Spirit makes a sinless life possible, absolute perfection is most likely to be realized after death.

blest," and "Jesus, keep me near the cross; / There a precious fountain, / Free to all a healing stream, / Flows from Calvary's mountain."

But worship could also be rambunctious. Persons receiving the second blessing were known to shout, preachers were dramatic in speaking style, and altar calls with loud weeping were common. Although they did not speak in tongues, Holiness people did emphasize the other gifts of the Spirit. Physical healings from disease were expected. From this distance, it seems that they were the Charismatics of their day.

The Holiness movement grew through the second half of the 1800s. It spawned new denominations, colleges, and other institutions all along the way. Among the new churches were the Free Methodist Church, the Salvation Army, the Church of God (Anderson, Indiana), the Wesleyan Church, and finally, after bishops of the Methodist Episcopal Church, South, began to discourage the Holiness movement, a large group departed to form the Church of the Nazarene.

Asbury College was founded in 1890, and out of this great school Asbury Theological Seminary was born. Literally dozens of other colleges, training schools, and camp meetings were born during the Holiness movement's heyday.

The Holiness Movement's Tradition of Service

As I've mentioned, the Holiness movement from the beginning tended to be overly austere and inflexible. There was a time when Martha would not wear lipstick, and we would never think of attending the most innocent movies. That weakness in the movement has been overemphasized, I think.

A more important characteristic of the Holiness movement has been its emphasis on *service*. The outstanding church historian George Marsden states, "In fact in the years from 1870–1890, before the rise of the Social Gospel, Holiness-minded evangelicals had . . . assumed leadership in American

Protestant work among the poor."[4] The Holiness people completely rejected the fundamentalist point of view that doing social work would lessen the emphasis on evangelism. Holiness proponents believed you could do both, and that's exactly what they did.

This is important, because Holiness adherents dominated Methodist (and many other denomination's) missionary enterprises for decades. Everywhere in the world they went, these thousands of ambassadors for Christ preached salvation *and* taught agriculture, gave medical treatment, and raised orphans. This kind of mission work became the pattern for all of America's large missionary efforts.

It's also good to remember that before theological liberals began emphasizing *only* social work, and fundamentalists began emphasizing *only* evangelism, the Holiness movement stressed *both*. This was once the pattern for all the Methodist and Wesleyan churches. It can be again.

Pentecostalism—Stepchild of the Holiness Movement

In the twentieth century Pentecostals/Charismatics and Holiness adherents have often been in hostile camps. So it's surprising to many to learn that Pentecostalism actually came out of the Holiness movement. In some ways it was a natural progression of the movement.

On January 1, 1901, an outbreak of tongues-speaking occurred at a Bible school run by Rev. Charles Fox Parham, near Topeka, Kansas. Parham took from this that speaking in unknown tongues, as described in 1 Corinthians 12 and other passages, ought to be a regular part of Christian worship.

Speaking in tongues should be an expected event, not an unusual oddity, Parham declared. For the next five years Parham spread this new Pentecostal theology through revival meetings in the midwest. In 1905 he moved to Houston and set up another Bible school, this time training a black preacher from the Holiness tradition named W. J. Seymour.[5]

Lamentably, Parham was not a believer in racial equality— he was an outright racist. Seymour was only allowed to listen to Parham's lectures from a chair set up outside the window. Yet even that was enough to convince him of the truth of the new Pentecostal message.

As with the other Holiness preachers who were attracted to Pentecostalism, Seymour taught that the "Baptism of the Spirit" which resulted in the gift of tongues was, in essence, a *second* Holy Spirit baptism. The first baptism resulted in sanctification, the second, spiritual gifts and power. Seymour was soon asked to pastor a Holiness mission church in Los Angeles.

The California church had been misinformed about Seymour's theology. They did not object to tongues-speaking *per se*, but when they learned how much their new pastor was stressing the gift of tongues, they revolted. He was soon fired. Ironically, Seymour had not been given the gift of tongues himself as yet. In 1906 Seymour began preaching regularly in homes, attracting seekers both black and white, Baptist, Holiness, Nazarene. There was enthusiasm, but as yet no actual speaking in tongues.

But on April 9, one of Seymour's congregants, a black man named Edward Lee, approached his pastor and reported a vision he had seen. He said the apostles had come to him and told him how to regain the gift of tongues in the modern age. The house church prayed that night and at last several of them, including Seymour, began speaking in an unknown tongue. Pentecostals view this prayer meeting as the beginning of their movement.[6]

Interest in the movement was immediate and enormous. Crowds overwhelmed the house they had been meeting in, so an empty building on seedy Azusa Street was located and turned into a meeting house. There the new church enjoyed ecstatic worship with tongues speaking, spontaneous preaching, and no offering taken.

One truly amazing thing happened! The color barrier was broken! Whites worshiped along with blacks and Mexicans without self-consciousness. There were even praying and weeping together at the altar. Visitors were sometimes scandalized by this intermingling. But in my mind, the love shown between the races proves the authenticity of Azusa Street far more than any spiritual gift could.

The theology of the movement was vague but catchy. Although the Holy Spirit had already been at work through his sanctifying power, now he had descended as in the first Pentecost, and the manifestation of tongues was the evidence. The second coming of Christ was expected momentarily. That's about as far as Seymour and his early followers got.

People came to check out the revival literally from around the country. Some accepted the racial integration, and some didn't. But the new doctrine of speaking in tongues held the whole thing together—for a time. It spread like wildfire. Within 14 years, 25 new Pentecostal denominations had sprouted around the country.[7]

The Pentecostal-Holiness Break

Within a few years of its beginning, Pentecostalism had become so controversial that few were neutral about it. You loved it or hated it. Signs of strain began early. In late 1906, Charles Parham, the original Pentecostalist, came to Los Angeles to look over the Azusa Street revival. He was appalled by what he saw, especially the mixing of the races.

Comparing the meetings to a "darkey revival," Parham wrote some of his impressions:

> . . . frequently a white woman, perhaps of wealth and culture, could be seen thrown back into the arms of a "buck nigger," and held tightly thus as she shivered and

shook in freak imitation of Pentecost. Horrible, awful shame![8]

Another early Pentecostalist invited to preach at Azusa Street was William H. Durham. After looking things over, Durham declared that Seymour's doctrine of three works of grace would not do. Of course he believed in the first one, being born again, and he accepted the third one, the Baptism of the Holy Spirit evidenced by speaking in tongues, with open arms.

But Durham rejected the second work of grace—the Wesleyan-Holiness doctrine of sanctification—as redundant and unnecessary. He said as much from the pulpit of the church. According to theologian Harvey Cox, "Seymour himself, and most of the members of the Azusa Street congregation, were devastated. Durham had undercut the entire theological rationale for the revival."[9] How could you experience a baptism of power, they felt, if you had not first had a baptism of cleansing?

Durham went on to found the Assemblies of God, which tended to attract former Baptists, Presbyterians, and others from the Reformed church tradition. In time, this non-Holiness branch of the Pentecostal movement came to dominate. Rather than tongues speaking and other fiery gifts being seen as a supplement to entire sanctification, as the first Pentecostals had viewed it, the Assemblies and other groups saw their "Baptism of the Holy Spirit" as a *substitute*.

Today, most Pentecostal and Charismatic churches trace their roots to this non-Holiness Pentecostalism. Notable exceptions are the Pentecostal Holiness Church, and the very large black denomination, the Church of God in Christ.

For the most part, those Pentecostals identifying with the Holiness emphasis continued to stress the Bible and heart purification. Some of the other Pentecostal groups, however, stumbled into heresy after heresy. Some began to perform water baptism in the name of Jesus only, rather than the Holy Trinity. Others insisted that God was now revealing himself through Pentecostal prophets, and that sometimes these new messages could contradict the Bible.

John Wesley would have been appalled by some of the excesses of the Pentecostals, just as he would have by the faithless liberalism of the United Methodist Church. Both errors would have been avoided if both groups would have guided themselves by the written Word of God and church tradition, as Wesley did so faithfully.

The Gift of Tongues Arousing Anger

Ever since the Charismatic movement arose in the mainline churches in the 1960s, I've been hearing about the movement "splitting churches." This is a most unfortunate charge. Sometimes it seems just, and sometimes not.

The issue in contention is often the gift of speaking in tongues. Though this is less common today than before, some Charismatics take the Pentecostal doctrine and insist that all Spirit-filled believers must exercise that particular gift.

If tongues speaking is controversial today, it was considered a scandal in the first years of the twentieth century. Pentecostals stood alone against virtually all other Christian groups in this practice. Even other Holy Spirit advocates harshly criticized Pentecostals for speaking in tongues.

E. Stanley Jones, the great Methodist Holiness missionary to India, was an outspoken critic of the spread of tongues. He wrote:

> To bind up the possession of the Holy Spirit with the possession of the gift of tongues is, to my mind, perhaps the greatest spiritual disaster that has struck this confused and groping age. Nothing would queer the gift of the Holy Spirit more quickly to thoughtful minds of this age than to reduce it to intelligibility.[10]

Methodist Holiness advocates like Jones were not saying that the gift of tongues could never be present. They did, however, violently oppose the notion that it must *always* be present.

The question must be asked: what happens to persons speaking in tongues? Is it authentic, or is it the product of mass hysteria or clever prompting? Stanley Jones, in the article quoted above, refers to some questionable techniques he had heard:

> A group will gather around the seeker and lay their hands on his head, and the seeker will be urged to use some foreign words he may know to start the flow. Or he will be instructed to hold his jaw loose and to let his tongue be limp. Or he will be asked to repeat the name of Jesus over and over and then urged to go faster and faster until he goes so fast that he begins to stammer.[11]

While I deplore these kind of manipulated maneuverings, I do not believe they are the whole story. Free Methodist pastor Howard Snyder has looked deeply into this question. In his book *The Divided Flame: Wesleyans and the Charismatic Renewal,* he examines many of the arguments against speaking in tongues, especially that it is based on irrationality, and responds this way:

> The truth, however, would appear to be that tongues-speaking is a nonrational but not necessarily irrational speech pattern which lies within the range of normal human behavior. Such tongues-speaking may or may not be prompted or inspired by the Holy Spirit. In some contexts it may be induced by other forces, whether psychological, social, or demonic. That is no more than we would admit for other rather extraordinary forms of behavior which in certain contexts we do not consider abnormal or pathological, including crying, screaming, shouting, or dancing. In this sense, [the Holiness experience of] "getting blessed" has many parallels to tongues-speaking. Sometimes it may be the

Spirit; other times it is clearly a manifestation of "the flesh."[12]

Regardless of the justice of the matter, the Holiness and Pentecostal camps were generally hostile to each other during the twentieth century. The Holiness proponents were thus isolated on both sides—from liberal-leaning Methodists and others who rejected any Holy Spirit experience subsequent to salvation on the one hand, and from Pentecostals, who now formed the cutting edge of Holy Spirit movements, on the other.

Other groups rejecting the Pentecostal message were groups sharing the dispensationalists' basic hostility toward spiritual gifts. The fundamentalist doctrine of dispensationalism, which teaches that the supernatural gifts died with the apostles, denies any possibility of tongues speaking. Baptists and the various Churches of Christ groups usually adopted the fundamentalists' basic hostility toward supernatural gifts.

However, all of this opposition to the Pentecostals did not halt their amazing growth. Consider the Chilean Methodist Church. In the early twentieth century a small group of Pentecostal dissidents withdrew from the American-planted Methodist Church in Chile. At that time the church had 5,000 to 6,000 members. The Pentecostals organized the Methodist Pentecostal Church.

In the years since, the new body has exploded in membership, to over 300,000. Meanwhile, the original Chilean Methodist Church is still stuck with fewer than 10,000 members. What made the difference? The original Chilean Methodist Church was just a miniature of the Methodist Church in the United States. Its emphasis was on education and structure. But as in the U.S., these fine things were not enough to prevent stagnation. On the other hand, the Pentecostals stressed Spirit-empowered evangelism and contemporary worship. It worked in Chile, and it works everywhere else in the world where it is tried.

Old, tradition-bound denominations are giving way to young, vigorous movements emphasizing Scripture and the power of the Holy Spirit. As stated in Chapter One, Pentecostals and Charismatics now number above 400,000,000—roughly eight percent of the world's population.

The Rise of the Charismatics

I spend a good deal of time in this book discussing the attributes of the modern Charismatic movement. Now I will give just a few words to explain how it arose.

The Charismatic movement is best understood as Pentecostalism brought into the traditional churches. Pentecostals emphasize the supernatural gifts of the Holy Spirit, adherence to Scripture, vigorous evangelism, and joyous worship. Charismatics stress the same things.

The movement sprang up in the 1950s through a number of Pentecostalist ministries operating within mainline churches. Examples are the Full Gospel Business Men's Association, the healing ministry of Agnes Sanford among Episcopalians, and United Methodist evangelist Tommy Tyson, to name just a few. When Pentecostal tent-meeting preacher Oral Roberts joined the Methodist ministry, it created a big impression. Many persons had a hand in forming the Charismatic movement, but no one individual can be called its "founder."[13]

In the United Methodist Church, the Lay Witness mission movement of the mid-1960s was heavily influenced by the new Charismatic emphasis. In Lay Witness missions, teams of enthusiastic laypersons would travel to a host church and merely share their personal testimonies. Many team members eagerly shared about the Charismatic experience. Many persons not only found Christ during the Lay Witness missions, they were also baptized in the Holy Spirit as well. The Lay Witness missions brought an amazing amount of new life—and not a little division—to churches across the denomination.

In just a few years Charismatics had a large presence in every nook and cranny of Protestantism—and Roman Catholicism too! Many Charismatics, frustrated by mainline church indifference or hostility to their movement, departed to form independent Charismatic congregations.

One positive development in the past 20 years has been a lessening of suspicion between Charismatic and non-Charismatic camps. Schools like Asbury Theological Seminary, which once strongly discouraged any talk of tongues speaking, now display much more tolerance. Every side seems to have grown.

The Toronto Movement Controversy

As it has grown and matured, the movement has spawned a number of new denominations. These are generally different from the old-line Pentecostal churches. More contemporary, more educated, and, significantly, usually much less aggressive about the necessity of speaking in tongues.

One fast-growing denomination is the Vineyard Christian Fellowship, founded by John Wimber. Before 1994, the Vineyard's biggest distinctive had been its "Signs and Wonders" seminars, where persons from around America would come to participate in the ministry of healing and other supernatural signs. This sophisticated, evangelism-oriented Charismatic body has generally been considered balanced and Scriptural.

Then, in January 1994, a new phenomenon erupted at one of the Vineyard's congregations, located in Toronto, Ontario. The Toronto Airport Vineyard held a series of revival services where the presence of the Holy Spirit was felt so strongly by participants that unusual new phenomena began occurring. Soon observers came flocking from around the world.

Dubbed the "Toronto Blessing," the movement became a nightly series that has stretched through this writing (about three years). The meetings are characterized by mass "slayings in the Spirit" and what has become known as "holy laughter."

Slayings in the Spirit have been experienced throughout the Pentecostal era, and even before. However, the Toronto Blessing has certainly brought them further into public view. Steve Beard, editor of *Good News* magazine, has even published a monograph titled *Thunderstruck: John Wesley and the Toronto Blessing*, which compares the supernatural phenomena surrounding both movements.[14]

But like the spontaneous faintings of the Wesleyan revival and the Second Great Awakening, the "slayings" of the Toronto Blessing immediately opened the movement to the charge of crowd manipulation. I have not journeyed to Toronto to observe the "blessing" in operation. But many of my friends and one of my sons have been at services sponsored by the movement. They describe the meetings as unusually intense Charismatic services— singing of praise songs that can last an hour or more, some speaking in tongues, a sermon. But there are also unfamiliar spiritual happenings that have become the trademark of the movement. My friend Dr. William Abraham of the Perkins School of Theology had a generally positive opinion of what he observed when he journeyed to Toronto. He describes some of what he saw:

> During the worship one or two developed uncontrollable shaking; this recurred in their case during the time of ministry. A few roared in agony, bending over, as if they were working through some terrible grief. One or two had uncontrollable jerking, bouncing up and down for half an hour. . . . Some people laughed uncontrollably on the floor for twenty minutes and more.[15]

One phenomenon Billy observed ranks with the strangest I have ever heard. Others have reported it elsewhere, so apparently it is becoming part of the movement:

> One evening one young man ended up on all fours, crawling and growling like a lion from one end of the building to another. Nobody was bothered by it. It was taken as

almost a natural occurrence between the individual and God, signifying the Lion of Judah's power and strength.[16]

The climax of the evening comes when participants needing prayer are encouraged to move to the front of the room. After sometimes being urged not to fight the Spirit, seekers tell their spiritual needs to the prayer team. Catchers position themselves behind each participant, and someone involved with the movement will lay his or her hands on the forehead of the person and pray for him or her according to the needs expressed. After a period of time, almost inevitably the seeker will fall backwards into the waiting arms of the catchers. The question is, was he or she pushed ever so slightly, giving the seeker the feeling that the Spirit was already acting? Some of the witnesses I've interviewed say yes, some say no.

Vineyard founder John Wimber himself cautioned Toronto Blessing enthusiasts early on that the movement, though a wonderful thing for Christian churches, did not qualify as a revival:

> I have no problem with the notion that people are being revived. I just have a problem with our using a term, that most evangelicals at least, reserve for that *phase* of revival that is an outpouring, not only *on* the church but *through* the church and *into* the community. The result [in revivals] is the salvation of thousands.[17]

The Toronto Movement quickly spread to churches all across America and Great Britain. A number of non-Pentecostal ministers and churches were affected. One was Presbyterian minister Dan Hendley, pastor of a Presbyterian church in America congregation in Florida. Under the ministry of Randy Clark, Hendley had a profound experience of God. He later noted, ". . . those things over which we have traditionally opposed the Charismatic movement are virtually non-existent at these meetings. Nobody is calling folks to be 'baptized in the Holy Ghost.' Nobody is preaching the necessity of tongues."[18]

As the months passed, amid growing concerns about animal noises and other phenomena not seen in the Bible, the Vineyard leadership issued a formal set of "guidelines." The guidelines seemed concerned mostly with preventing excesses. For instance, guideline three states:

> We would like people to be known as "zealous Christian workers" rather than "roarers" or "shakers." We do not want manifestations to be a mark of spirituality. Rather, the fruit and gifts of the Spirit and a godly character should attest to true spirituality.[19]

More Controversy Surrounding the Toronto Movement

In February, 1995, the Toronto Movement held a brief series of meetings in Wilmore, Kentucky, home of the Asbury institutions. All the usual things happened at the meetings, but the reaction from the Wilmore community was anything but usual. Many in town embraced the meetings as a fresh touch of the Spirit. But many others rejected it completely. Once again, a division between the Charismatic and Holiness believers grew wide.

Asbury Seminary president Maxie Dunnam took a neutral stance on the Toronto Movement itself, stating that he believed in miracles and healings. However, in the interest of preserving campus unity, he decided to cancel a seminary chapel service planned by the movement adherents.

Dr. John Oswalt, a long-time ATS professor, compared the Toronto Movement approach to "magic." That is, actions we people take resulting in some guaranteed blessing from God. "There was . . . ," he wrote to the faculty, "no emphasis upon repentance and confession. Why? Because in a magical conception, none is necessary. One need only be brought into physical, or mental, contact with the source of power and the desired result will be achieved." Oswalt compared this thinking to the Holiness doctrine, which stresses the transformation of character.[20]

By late 1995 John Wimber and the Vineyard national leadership felt uncomfortable enough with the direction the movement was going that they issued what might be seen as a warning statement:

> We cannot at any time endorse, encourage, offer theological justification or biblical proof-texting for any exotic practices that are extrabiblical [i.e., not mentioned in Scripture]. Neither can these practices be presented as criteria for true spirituality or as a mark of true renewal.[21]

In January 1996 the Vineyard denomination broke with the Toronto Airport Vineyard. Spokesman Todd Hunter explained that the move came after pastor John Arnott had been warned to de-emphasize the unusual phenomena. "We value the dignity of the individual," he explained. "Somebody doing bizarre manifestations, being brought up on stage to do them is not, we think, very dignified. In our mind it's exploitive."

Conclusions

Obviously the history of Pentecostalism in America is an unfolding one. It is often very difficult to discern which Holy Spirit movements are authentic, which ones are manipulated, and which ones are a combination of both.

We must remember to guard the truth and pay attention to theology. But we must also be open to new things the Holy Spirit is doing. How can we tell if it is really the Holy Spirit? "You shall know them by their fruits," says the Bible.

Notes

1   George M. Marsden, *Fundamentalism and American Culture* (London: Oxford University Press, 1980), p. 73.

2   Charles Finney, *Lectures on Systematic Theology*, J. H. Fairchild, ed. (1878. reprint. Grand Rapids: Eerdmans Publishing Co., n.d.), 407.

3 Marsden, p. 79.

4 Ibid., p. 81.

5 Howard A. Snyder with Daniel V. Runyon, *The Divided Flame: Wesleyans and the Charismatic Renewal* (Grand Rapids: Zondervan Publishing House, 1986), p. 40.

6 Harvey Cox, *Fire From Heaven* (Reading, Mass.: Addison-Wesley Publishing Company, 1995), p. 56.

7 Snyder, p. 42.

8 Cox, p. 61.

9 Ibid., p. 62.

10 "Authentic Proofs of the Holy Spirit," E. Stanley Jones. Untraced.

11 Ibid., page 4.

12 Snyder and Runyon, p. 81.

13 Peter Hocken, *The Glory and the Shame: Reflections on the 20th Century Outpouring of the Holy Spirit* (Guildford, Surrey, UK: Eagle, 1994), pp. 34–35.

14 Steve Beard, *Thunderstruck: John Wesley and the Toronto Blessing* (Wilmore, Ky.: Thunderstruck Communications, 1996).

15 William J. Abraham, "Awakening in Toronto: Personal Report and Reflections," unpublished paper, 1994, p. 4.

16 Ibid.

17 John Wimber, "Season of New Beginnings," *Vineyard Reflections*, May/June 1994, p. 3.

18 Dan D. Hendley, "Pastoral Letter to the Members of Covenant Presbyterian Church Concerning the Renewal Meetings at the Tabernacle," February 14, 1995, p. 9.

19 Board Report, Association of Vineyard Churches, September/October 1994, p. 2.

20 John Oswalt, untitled report for Asbury Theological Seminary faculty, undated.

21 Sharon Waxman, "Filled with the Ho-Ho-Ho Spirit," *The Washington Post*, January 2, 1996, p. C1.

CHAPTER 8

How to Practice the Gifts of the Spirit

Some Scriptural and Practical Guidelines

he Bible never says, "By their gifts you will recognize them." But it does say, "By their fruit you will recognize them" (Matthew 7:16). No one gift is the necessary evidence of the Spirit-filled life. Holiness of heart and life is the only certain evidence of the fullness of the Spirit.

On the other hand, it is certainly possible to squash the works of the Spirit, including the gifts. During the past several years those who have not made a place for spiritual gifts have often felt threatened by those who do. But the Scriptures must be allowed to speak for themselves and to guide us in our conclusions. We cannot discount the gifts of the Spirit merely because they may make us feel uncomfortable.

In the history of the Christian church, there has never been such widespread interest in the biblical teaching about this vital aspect of the Christian life.

A spiritual gift refers to a supernatural enabling of the Holy Spirit which equips a Christian for his or her work of service and ministry. Scriptures distinguish between the gift of the Spirit, which is the birthright of every Christian, and the *gifts* of the Spirit. Spiritual fruit is the description of who we *are*; rather, who the Holy Spirit has made us. Spiritual gifts, on the other hand, describe what we *do* through God's power.

Spiritual fruit has to do with our relationships and the spiritual quality of our lives. Spiritual gifts have to do with our calling and function in ministry.

A spiritual gift is a supernatural ability or capacity given by God to enable the Christian to minister, serve and praise.

The New Testament, especially the letters of Paul, teach extensively on the gifts of the Spirit. The major passages are: Romans 12:6–8, 1 Corinthians 12:4–11, 1 Corinthians 12:28, and Ephesians 4:11.

Some additional passages are 1 Corinthians 1:5–7, 12:29–30, 13:8, 2 Corinthians 8:7; 1 Thessalonians 5:20; 1 Timothy 4:14; 2 Timothy 1:6–7; Hebrews 2:4; 1 Peter 4:10–11. Also, 1 Corinthians 14:1–25.

Kenneth Kinghorn, in his book *Gifts of the Spirit* (quoted extensively in this chapter), lists five basic principles regarding spiritual gifts:[1]

First, "God imparts spiritual gifts according to his divine grace; they cannot be earned through human merit."

Second, "God gives spiritual gifts according to his own discretion; he is not bound to man's wishes."

This means that it is not appropriate for a Christian to insist that God grant him or her any one gift. We may desire the gift of prophecy or speaking in tongues. But the Bible says the Spirit gives these supernatural gifts "to each man, just as he determines" (1 Corinthians 12:11). The writer to the Hebrews declared, "God also testified to it [salvation] by signs, wonders and various miracles, and gifts of the Holy Spirit distributed according to his will" (Hebrews 2:4).

However, Paul does say we should "eagerly desire the greater gifts" (1 Corinthians 12:13) and "eagerly desire spiritual gifts" (1 Corinthians 14:1).

The third principle Kinghorn mentions is: "God wills that every Christian exercise spiritual gifts; these divine enablings are not limited to a few believers."

It is a tragedy that many churches embrace only certain gifts such as healing or speaking in tongues and center much of their corporate life around those few gifts. It is an equal blight, however, that many mainline churches refuse to allow any gifts at all into their worship and ministry. The healthy, vital, growing church needs all the spiritual gifts described in the New Testament.

Kinghorn's fourth principle is, "God provides gifts for the purpose of ministry and service; they are not given in order to draw attention to man or to satisfy his ego."

Doesn't that seem obvious? Yet it is not, for the history of the contemporary church is filled with pitiful examples of ministers and other leaders claiming to have gifts of healing, prophecy, or apostleship, even though their actions sometimes put these claims to the lie. Even when a minister has had a marvelous gift, sometimes great harm has been done by the spiritual immaturity of the person involved. In other words, the giftee was not worthy of the gift. Let us pray it is not so with us.

Fifth, "God intends that the ministry of the church be accomplished through spiritual gifts; human talents are not adequate for spiritual ministry."

The gifts of the Spirit may be neglected for many reasons. People may not be aware they possess these supernatural giftings. Or, they resist using them; perhaps they are afraid. In many churches, spiritual gifts are frowned upon, so Christians there may "sit" on any gifts they have.

Kinghorn writes that it is not necessary to be aware of exercising gifts in order to do so. Someone may have the gift of administration, for example, making an outstanding chairman of the church board, without being aware that this "talent" is actually a gift from above.

With that background given, we'll now look at the gifts one by one, starting with the *enabling gifts*. A list of these gifts is found in Ephesians 4:11–12.

Paul lists five enabling gifts: "It was he who gave some to be apostles, some to be prophets, some to be evangelists, and some to be pastors and teachers, to prepare God's people for works of service, so that the body of Christ may be built up" (Ephesians 4:11–12).

Apostleship

The word *apostle* means "a messenger" or "one who is sent forth." Are there apostles still today? Obviously, the term was first used to describe the hand-picked disciples of Jesus who later spread the Gospel throughout the ancient world. These first missionaries were only called apostles if they personally knew Jesus of Nazareth. Paul claimed the title of apostle because of his miraculous vision, where Christ appeared to him on the road to Damascus.

There will be no more of these first apostles, these founders of the church. Yet Paul listed apostleship as one of the gifts of the Spirit. If the gift operates today, what can it mean?

I believe a modern apostle is someone who takes the message of Christ across cultural boundaries, who plants churches, who pioneers works for God. Missionaries often have the gift of apostleship, I believe.

Prophecy

Today the church is desperate for leaders who are gifted in reading the signs of the times and giving a corrective word. We've heard enough of men's opinions—we need a word from the Lord!

The Bible is packed with prophets, especially in the Old Testament. These men and women acted as God's mouthpieces to the leaders and cultures of the day. Sometimes they predicted the future, but usually those predictions were based on present-day spiritual realities (i.e., God will destroy Israel if it does not repent). Mostly, prophecy is about correctly interpreting and delivering the word of God. That word could be an internal nudging of the Spirit, or it could come straight from the Bible.

Too often in recent times liberal church leaders have described some of their blatantly political statements as "prophetic." I believe that making such claims for yourself is like playing with spiritual fire. Woe be to you if you turn out to be a false prophet!

Who have been post-biblical prophets? Clearly Martin Luther, with his message of cleaning up church corruption and error, would qualify. More recently, the names of Charles Colson and Father Richard John Neuhaus come to mind.

In 1 Corinthians 14, Paul gave the following guidelines for evaluating prophecy. According to Ken Kinghorn, the guidelines should be interpreted this way:

1. Prophecy will edify or build up a congregation.
2. Prophecy will encourage and impart life.
3. Prophecy will console believers and draw them toward God in Christian unity.[2]

Paul wrote, "Eagerly desire spiritual gifts, especially the gift of prophecy" (1 Corinthians 14:1).

Evangelism

The word *evangelism*, in the original Greek, should be interpreted "to proclaim the good news." As a full-time evangelist for more than 30 years, I am of course very interested in the evangelistic work of the church. Witnessing to your faith in Christ is not the work of the few but of the many. When

Jesus gave his disciples the Great Commission, "Go into all the world and make disciples," he was giving instructions to *all* his followers.

I am bothered that many view sharing their faith as some sort of unsavory spiritual obligation. But if you really believe the Gospel is *good news*, why withhold it from your friends, neighbors, and associates? Would you fail to tell someone if he or she had inherited a million dollars?

And yet, there is such a thing as a gift of evangelism. Persons possessing that gift have a supernatural desire and ability to win persons to Christ. A great example of someone with the gift of evangelism is E. Stanley Jones, the great missionary to India (and the rest of the world).

When Jones applied to the Methodist mission board during his senior year at Asbury College (1906–1907), one question he was asked concerned whether he had enjoyed any success in winning souls to Christ. He answered that in his four years of preaching revival on weekends and summers, he believed he could account for at least 500 conversions!

Shepherding

The biblical term of *shepherd* has been abused by those who would use their spiritual positions to gain power over the lives of their people. Actually, Paul uses the term interchangeably with *elder* and *bishop*. What they all mean is simply pastor—they are our modern-day ministers.

The importance of *shepherd* being listed as a gift of the Holy Spirit is clear. The ministry is not a profession—it's a calling. I've often said that the church has too many "daddy-called preachers." America's landscape is filled with churches wrecked by pastors who did not possess the gift of the Spirit necessary to do the job.

No one should become a minister of the Gospel without the call—the gift of shepherding. On the other hand, persons experiencing that call have no choice but to surrender to it.

Teaching

Teaching is a necessary role in the church, and an important gift of the Spirit (Ephesians 4:11). Persons having this gift make the faith come alive to believers. They can deepen our knowledge of Scripture. They can help us apply our beliefs to our everyday lives.

Our Sunday school teacher slots should be filled with persons possessing this spiritual gift (not just by people willing to volunteer).

We now examine the serving gifts.

The Word of Wisdom

Ken Kinghorn says, "The word of wisdom . . . enables one to apply spiritual truth to a concrete situation in a specially anointed way so that others recognize the truth that has been spoken."[3]

This is not the same thing as human cleverness or mental dexterity. Someone who is "wise" in the handling of stocks and bonds may be totally lacking in the wisdom which is given by the Holy Spirit. How many times a church or Christian organization has gotten into trouble because someone having a gift of wisdom was not present to show the way!

Of course, spiritual wisdom does not cancel out scholarship. Jesus and Paul were men of extraordinary learning. God's wisdom makes use of our preparation.

The Word of Knowledge

This gift is often practiced (perhaps too often) in Charismatic circles. But it *is* a legitimate gift of the Spirit. When Jesus told the woman at the well about her sordid past, she knew only God could have told him this. If the Lord wants to reveal some information or insight that human understanding cannot fathom, he uses a word of knowledge. This is a valuable gift for counseling.

Faith

Naturally it takes a measure of faith to be a Christian at all, but the gift of faith gives a Christian the power to believe at a heightened level. The resulting faith can lead to a deeper prayer life. This is a marvelous gift.

Gifts of Healing

Persons trained in the Methodist holiness tradition, such as myself, have generally taught that divine healing is a multifaceted matter. Some are healed one way, some another. God does finally heal everyone who believes; however, not always in the way we expect.

Kinghorn lists five ways God heals:

1. God heals instantly and directly.
2. God heals gradually through the process of nature.
3. God heals through medical science.
4. God gives grace to suffer redemptively by healing our attitudes.
5. God heals in the resurrection.[4]

If God heals in many ways, those who possess the gift of healing can expect that many they pray for will not become physically well. Yet God will extend his healing grace to the sufferer through the faith of the healer.

Paul did not receive physical healing for the unnamed illness which plagued him. But Paul reports that God had given him the grace to withstand his problem. I hope the church will soon rid itself of any tendency to blame the sick for their illnesses (e.g., they did not have enough faith to be healed). After all, Lazarus was raised from the dead only to face death a second time. All of us will die, but God heals in the resurrection and in our attitudes.

Workings of Miracles

The term *miracles* used in the Gospels can also be translated as "attesting signs." These acts, such as feeding the 5,000, had a purpose, and that was to prove that Jesus truly was sent by God. Of course, Jesus seemed to use his miraculous powers to heal at times just because he felt compassion for the sick, as when he reached out to Blind Bartimaeus.

Again, Kinghorn offers valuable insight. "Although God continues to work miracles in our time," he states, "miracles are not required to validate the Christian message. Changed lives remain the greatest possible demonstration of God's miraculous working in our world."[5]

Authentic miracles can bring unbelievers to faith and strengthen the faith of Christians. However, exaggerated or dishonest "miracles" can destroy faith when they are discovered. It is critical that Christians resist the temptation to chase after the bizarre, the sensational. When God wishes to bless his church with an "attesting sign," he can do it without prompting.

Discernment

In this book I have taken pains to suggest that the mainline churches must be open to the new work God is doing through the Charismatic movement if they hope to thrive. Yet, I have also pointed out some of the problems Charismatics and Pentecostals often experience: too much reliance on emotion and too little regard for the traditions of the church. Wesley, while always being open to a fresh word from God, stubbornly clung to orthodoxy.

The only way the church can venture into new spiritual territory without losing its way is by having great spiritual discernment. Is what this leader or that self-appointed prophet says an authentic word from God? Is a suggested new doctrine truly in line with Scripture? The spiritual gift of discernment allows a Christian to answer these questions using God's insights. Pray for the gift of discernment!

Helps and Serving

Ken Kinghorn describes these as vital "background" gifts. Often people who help keep the church running smoothly and see to the needs of people think they have no spiritual gift at all. Far from it! What a world it would be if compassion and service to individuals died out.

Administration and Giving Aid

Two closely related spiritual gifts are administration (1 Corinthians 12:28) and giving aid (Romans 12:8). The Methodist tradition has always stressed careful administration and management. But that's not necessarily the same thing as possessing the gift of administration. Someone having this gift is able to see how the Lord would organize the church to meet changing circumstances and unusual challenges. If you have the gift of administration, you cannot be married to the past. By this measure, the mainline churches have lately exhibited little of this giftedness.

Giving aid in the Greek translates as "he who provides leadership in giving aid." A church treasurer ought to possess this spiritual gift, for it gives the bearer the ability to coordinate the church's resources.

Exhortation

Is this the same thing as preaching? It can be, but preaching can also involve teaching and evangelism. To exhort is to convince people of a truth, to "rally the troops," to lead by your words. Men and women with the gift of exhortation often find themselves in the role of pastor, counselor, and teacher. Many times I have complained that some pastors preach what amounts to "rosewater essays." That is, they use soft, soothing language to say very little. Probably they are mismatched for the job. The gift of exhortation adds starch to your message.

Giving

Sometimes I hear people say, "All I can do is give. I wish I could do more." Yet giving itself is a spiritual gift, and people who have been given it give generously and cheerfully.

Compassion

"Compassion transcends both natural human sympathy and normal Christian concern," says Kinghorn, "enabling one to sense in others a wide range of human emotions and then provide a supportive ministry of caring."[6]

The Gift of Tongues and the Interpretation of Tongues

Since the subject of tongues has been addressed several places throughout this book, little needs to be repeated here.

We first learn of speaking in tongues in Acts 2. On the day of Pentecost believers from around the ancient world were filled with the Holy Spirit and began speaking in foreign languages they had never learned. Later, some Christians began speaking in *glossolalia*, non-understandable speech which is sometimes referred to as a "prayer language" (Romans 8:26). In either case, one's prayer is addressed to God, not to other people (1 Corinthians 14:28).

If speaking in tongues is exercised publicly, Paul insists that an interpreter is required. Interpreting tongues is in itself a spiritual gift. Using it, the interpreter can discern what God is trying to communicate to the church through the tongues speaker.

Notes

1   This chapter, while not copying, does follow the outline of and relies heavily on Dr. Kenneth Kinghorn's books, *The Gifts of the Spirit* (Nashville: Abingdon Press, 1976) and *Discovering Your Spiritual Gifts* (Grand Rapids: Zondervan Publishing House, 1981). I am much indebted to Dr. Kinghorn for his insights, as well as his permission.

2   *The Gifts of the Spirit*, p. 49.

3   Ibid., p. 61.

4   Ibid., p. 68.

5   Ibid., p. 74.

6   Ibid., p. 92.

CHAPTER 9

Finding the Will of God through the Holy Spirit

God's Way of Communicating

*I*t has been the common experience of committed Christians to have been led by the Holy Spirit. The book of Acts tells us how Paul was forbidden by the Holy Spirit to preach in Asia and was called to Macedonia (Acts 16:6–10). Paul was led by God when he was seeking his will.

Some never hear the voice of God because they seldom listen, stop and wait. They do not have a quiet time and therefore, make serious mistakes because they are relying on human wisdom rather than divine direction.

Let us be cautious here. It is not always easy to know God's will. Some sincere people are always saying God told me this or God said that. And sometimes it turns out to be wrong. God never makes a mistake, but our reception may be imperfect. We must always use the language of humility; e.g., "I sense this is God's will."

Then how can we know the will of God for our lives?

The Spirit Reveals His Will through the Scriptures

Some never hear the "voice" of God because they seldom read the Word of God. The Lord will never lead us contrary to his revealed Word. If you want to know what the Lord would have you do concerning your marriage, read the Bible. If you want to know what your attitude should be concerning others, read the Scriptures. If you want to know God's will concerning personal morality, read his Word.

There is not a proof text for every situation we may face. However, the Bible gives principles that help guide us in all circumstances. For instance, the Scriptures do not explicitly teach total abstinence from all alcoholic beverages, but when we see what the alcohol traffic is doing to persons, families and societies, who can doubt that total abstinence is the best Christian witness?

The Word does not condemn enforced legal segregation, but it does teach us that every person is created in the image of God and is of infinite worth. Therefore, anything that dehumanizes is contrary to the teaching of Scripture. The principles of Scripture can be applied to almost every situation.

We are inspired to do the will of God by reading his Word. For some of us, the problem is not in knowing the Lord's will but in the desire to do it. When I read my Bible, my heart burns within me, and I find I want to be used in his kingdom.

Dwight L. Moody is quoted as saying, "The Bible will keep you from sin, or sin will keep you from the Bible." Satan plagues the believers with doubt and temptation. The Scriptures feed our faith and strengthen us in the hour of temptation. Remember, Jesus answered the temptations of the devil with Scripture. God reveals his will and inspires us to do it through his Word.

There are occasions when a particular text stands out. You may have read that passage many times before but in this situation the Holy Spirit speaks to you through this text. I recall when God spoke to my need through Psalm 103. When I was recovering from my hunting accident, wondering if my right arm and hand might be paralyzed for the rest of my life, the promise came, "He . . . heals all my diseases; he redeems my life from the pit . . . so that my youth is renewed like the eagle's." The Spirit spoke to me through this word, encouraged me and inspired faith and confidence.

The Spirit Leads Us through the Counsel of Christian Friends

I was pastor in a West Texas city. As a young man, I was determined to do something that I thought was God's will. Undoubtedly, if I had followed that course, it would have brought irreparable damage to my ministry. In the zeal and immaturity of my youth, I was convinced it was the right thing to do. My parents heard about my impending decision and traveled more than 500 miles to visit with me about it. They had not been in my home five minutes until I realized how foolish the thing I was about to do was. The Lord had spoken to me through my parents.

As a young minister I would sometimes have problems in my congregation that seemed like mountains. I would visit my district superintendent, who was a mature man with a strong faith and rich experience. He would offer me a soda pop and take one himself. My friend would sip on one small cola for more than an hour. In his presence there was calmness and assurance, and I could see things in proper perspective. The mountains of problems in my church became mole hills. The Holy Spirit spoke to me through that good man.

However, there is danger in seeking the counsel of others. God may want you to do a difficult and unpopular thing. A nominal Christian is never going to think you should make a sacrifice, but that may be just what you should do. In discerning God's will you should seek the counsel of mature, Spirit-filled Christians.

Circumstances Can Help the Christian Know God's Will

The Lord opens and shuts doors. While I was a college student, I was asked to supply a new neighborhood church until conference. I wanted to be appointed the permanent pastor of that church so very much. My wife and I knelt on our knees and asked the Lord to move our district superintendent's heart to give us that church. He did not do it.

Instead, I was appointed to a country preaching circuit. That year we had a great revival. In one week's time there were 41 conversions, and I baptized 39, mostly adults. That pastoral charge led the district in professions of faith and new members. The Lord knew I was not ready for that city church, but he opened the door to the rural appointment where I was mightily used by him.

It may be through a need that the Spirit will speak to you. Perhaps you are concerned about something in your church, choir, Sunday school, youth group—it may be the Lord is calling you to serve in that need. It could be that in your community there is a problem that has burdened you. Have you considered that God may be calling you with that need?

The Lord reveals his will with the talents he has given us. Some Christians have experienced disappointment and frustration because they have not dedicated their talents to God.

There was a beautiful young girl who could sing like an angel. Some of the wealthy congregations in her hometown often gave her honorariums to sing solos for their worship services. Her pastor secured a scholarship for her to enroll in one of our church-related colleges and dedicate her talent to the Lord. But she didn't take this wonderful opportunity, nor did she ever find a way to dedicate herself and her voice to God. She drifted away from the church and later found herself in serious trouble.

I have often wondered how different her life might have been if she had obeyed the Holy Spirit's call.

I have on occasion found it helpful to put out a fleece (i.e., ask the Lord to do something to indicate his will). There is danger in this. A person may be tempted to bargain with God. Shortly before I went into the Navy during World War II I thought I was in love with a beautiful college girl. One night after a date I was walking home and praying. I said, "Lord, if you will give me Punch, I will preach the gospel." The Lord didn't give me Punch, thank goodness, but I am preaching the gospel. One must not attempt to bargain with God. This you must never do!

Our obedience to his will should never be conditional. We should say with Job, "Though he slay me, yet will I hope in him" (Job 13:15). For the committed Christian, to know his will is to do it. However, it is not always easy to discern the will of the Lord. At times it has been helpful for me to ask God to do something that would indicate his will.

In 1965, I was having a difficult time trying to decide if I should go into evangelism. I had a wife and five children. It's not easy to go on the road as an evangelist with that kind of responsibility. One of the leaders of my conference told me I needed to see a psychiatrist. He said I had a bright future in the pastoral ministry and was about to blow it all. I was afraid he might be correct. If I went into evangelism, I wanted to do it right. I felt that I should have musicians, a magazine, follow-up programs, a youth ministry and offices. All this cost money, and I did not have any. I asked the Lord to supply my Association with $10,000 if he wanted me to be an evangelist—not as a condition for doing his will, but the assurance of his blessing. On Christmas Eve of 1965, an outstanding Christian layman gave me a check for $12,500 for the Ed Robb Evangelistic Association. I responded to the Spirit's call, and he has blessed me in a marvelous way.

The Lord Guides Us with a Still Small Voice

In Acts 16, it is recorded that Paul had a vision. Sometimes in unusual circumstances, God speaks to us through a dream or a vision.

J. B. Phillips, the outstanding translator of the New Testament, tells of such an experience in his book, *A Ring of Truth*. He was going through the dark night of his soul. The world was looking to the great J. B. Phillips to write another book, and he had nothing to say. The radical theologians in the mid-1960s were teaching that God was dead. Dr. Phillips was afraid they might be right. He apparently was in deep depression.

In this hour of need, C. S. Lewis appeared to him one night. Dr. Lewis had been dead for more than a year! Phillips had not been thinking about him and had only met him on one occasion. He gave J. B. Phillips a message and was gone. A few nights later C. S. Lewis appeared again and gave the identical message and disappeared. Dr. J. B. Phillips arose and wrote what many consider to be his greatest book.[1]

This was no seance! Dr. Phillips was not seeking to talk to the dead through a medium. That is of the devil. God was using a dream to send a message. Some would contend that all this could be explained psychologically. That's all right. I have no problem with this explanation. God is also the author of psychology.

I had a similar experience. I was going through a most difficult period; Satan was plaguing me. My father was a dedicated Christian, and I was very close to him. I had not dreamed of him once since his death several years before. One night he came to me in a dream and gave me a message. He returned several nights later and gave me the identical message. I considered it a message from God, and I obeyed.

But this is the unusual, the extraordinary way the Lord reveals his will. Ordinarily, he speaks to us with the still small voice. There is the thought. We cannot escape it. It is in keeping with God's Word and the best of Christian experience. At the thought, our heart burns within us. I remember going to revival services as a teenager. My heart burned. I felt that I should preach. There was the tug of the Spirit and there was no peace until I said yes.

Where the Lord leads, he will bless. It is not always easy, but he will provide the resources. Seek his will, and you will likely find it. Do his will, and he will prosper you in his kingdom.

Note

1   J. B. Phillips, *Ring of Truth: A Translator's Testimony* (New York: Macmillan, 1967), pp. 118–119.

CHAPTER 10

Charismatic Excess and Traditionalist Prejudice

Time to Practice Tolerance and Grace

*A*fter reading this far, some of my readers will probably question my earlier statement that I am not a Charismatic. It is true that while I have never spoken in tongues, I am sympathetic to the movement. In a way, it seems to me that John Wesley was more Charismatic than I am. His meetings were characterized by slayings in the Spirit, shouting, and shaking, while mine have not been.

Some of my friends have expressed concern about the Charismatic movement. They are afraid it will split the church. Others react strongly to the "manifestations" of the Spirit, believing it is emotional fanaticism.

My response is that the danger I see in the church is not emotionalism but lethargy. As I travel over the church I see decline and decay. Nevertheless, the traditionalists are singing, "I will not be moved."

Undoubtedly, mistakes have been made by my fellow traditionalists as well as my Charismatic brothers and sisters. I want to share some honest observations about both and offer some modest suggestions.

We had better learn to accept each other. Our opponents are the secularists and pagans who would destroy the church. We should say with John Wesley, "If thine heart is as my heart . . . give me thine hand." All believers should be allies in the battle for the hearts and minds of lost souls.

Advice for the Church Today

Contemporary worship styles are fine, even necessary, but often they lack theological depth. The great historic hymns of the church are rich in meaning and scriptural truth. While scriptural choruses can bless and inspire, hymns should not be neglected. Look at the Wesley hymns as a model. They are Christ-centered and full of scriptural truth and depth.

Dead formalism should be avoided, but there is value in using the liturgy of the church. It helps to keep worship Christ-centered and scripturally based. We must not be a slave to any form of worship, and we should always be open to the Spirit's serendipities. We impoverish ourselves when we totally reject all liturgy.

I have noticed that many churches no longer affirm their faith with the ecumenical creeds (Apostles', Nicene, Athanasian). This is to be regretted. We need to be reminded of the central truths of the faith. Perhaps this is one reason why many churches have strayed from orthodoxy.

It seems that most Charismatics and evangelicals lack a proper appreciation for the sacraments of the church—baptism and the Lord's Supper. Many are literalists in interpreting other parts of Scripture but are inclined to neglect or discount the importance of the sacraments as a means of grace, which is clearly taught in Scripture. A high priority should be given to the celebration of the sacraments.

The Christian faith cannot be separated from the body of Christ—the church. Spirit-filled believers will never make an impact on the church until they demonstrate loyalty and commitment. Individualism is the plague of renewal movements. Too many persons are looking for that "perfect" church. They keep moving from church to church, wanting to be fed. This contributes to instability in the church as well as in believers. Our witness is needed in traditional nominal churches.

Heretical Teachings and Exaggerated Claims

One of the most dangerous heresies in the church today is the "prosperity gospel." It is ironic that this is being preached when the symbol of the Christian faith is the cross, an instrument of sacrifice and suffering. The "name it and claim it" message is misleading. Some say God's children deserve the best, and material blessings will follow spiritual commitment. Our Lord said, "If anyone would come after me, he must deny himself and take up his cross and follow me" (Matthew 16:24).

There are persons who are always saying, "The Lord told me," or "the Lord said." This can lead to arrogance and spiritual pride. This makes them infallible in their own eyes. How could one disagree with the Lord? Yet the language of humility is, "I sense the Lord is leading," or, "I believe it is the Lord's will." You may be mistaken, but the Lord is never wrong. Your reception may be faulty. Many have fallen into error and followed a disastrous path, believing the Lord had spoken to them. In seeking the will of God we should ask for the counsel of mature Christian friends and make sure our decisions are in harmony with the Word of God.

Charismatics should be cautious about making claims they cannot substantiate. Exaggeration only leads to discrediting the authentic. During the great Indonesian revival there were reports of persons being raised from the dead and many astonishing miracles. An evangelical Christian magazine sent reporters to Indonesia to investigate the claims. They found them to be greatly exaggerated. This led to sincere questions about the authenticity of the revival.

I believe the Indonesian revival was one of the great movements of the Holy Spirit in the twentieth century. Many miracles undoubtedly took place, the greatest of them being the salvation of tens of thousands of souls. The exaggerations only weakened the witness.

It seems to me that the Charismatic renewal does not adequately stress holiness of life. Experience is too often emphasized to the neglect of ethics. I once counseled with a young woman who professed the gift of tongues and other gifts of the Spirit. She was living a boldly sinful life, indulging in numerous adulterous affairs, while testifying to the baptism of the Holy Spirit. I questioned how she could be filled with the Spirit and still living in sin. I said to her, "Remember, it's the *Holy* Spirit."

Spirit-filled Christians should be good citizens. In our zeal to win souls to Christ we must not neglect this world. Someone has got to lead in our civic responsibilities. Too often, it is left to the secularist. Part of our Christian witness should be service to the community. Our interest should not be narrow but should include all that makes for a healthy environment and a better world.

Traditionalist Prejudice

As a traditionalist I would be afraid to oppose what may be a genuine movement of the Holy Spirit. Mainline churches with their traditionalist mentality are declining almost everywhere. The baby boomers, baby busters, and the X generation are deserting the traditionalist churches in growing numbers. In 1957, 40 percent of the members of the United Methodist Church were over 50 years of age. In 1994, 61.4 percent of the members were over 50 years old. The numbers are similar in all the mainline churches. The Charismatics and Pentecostals are booming with growing numbers of young adults and youth. Shouldn't we take note and learn some lessons?

Many traditionalists resist contemporary expressions of worship. They insist on classical music and seventeenth- and eighteenth-century hymns. It seems that their worship services are planned by classical musicians who have lost touch with the average person in the pew. Perhaps we should seek a balance between the classical and the contemporary.

Traditionalists are conservative in style, and are therefore suspicious of the new or innovative. But we simply cannot do things like we did in 1950. The world has changed, and we will become more flexible or we will decline and even become irrelevant in the next generation. We must be open to changes in worship styles and church government. The gospel never changes, but styles and cultures do. We must never compromise the essence of the faith, but we should search for better ways to communicate it.

The baby boomers and baby busters respond negatively to excessive ritual. They prefer a free style of worship. Robes turn them off.

Traditionalists are loyal to the connectional church. Denominational loyalty is high on their list of priorities. The new generation's interest is usually limited to the local church. Apportionments for the general church will increasingly be criticized and even opposed.

Emotional expression is criticized by the traditionalist. They are afraid of wild fire and fanaticism. The danger I see in most mainline churches is no fire. The services are lacking in enthusiasm and the preaching in zeal. Almost anything meaningful touches our emotions. Ritual is no substitute for personal experience.

Traditionalists usually prefer order to spiritual manifestations. In contrast, I had a friend who often prayed before the worship service, "Lord, may something happen today that is not in the bulletin." We cannot program the Holy Spirit. Perhaps we have been guilty of trying to domesticate the Holy Spirit. In the great revivals of the past there have been remarkable manifestations of the Spirit. This is likely to happen today when renewal comes.

Historical Examples of Religious Enthusiasm

As I have made clear, the physical manifestations of religious excitement—falling, running, jerking, crying out, loss of consciousness—were not unknown to Jonathan Edwards, George Whitefield, and the Wesleys. The name "shouting Methodists" may have come from northern Ireland, where the more uninhibited Methodists were known as "Irish Shouters."[1]

Peter Cartwright, a frontier Methodist preacher, tells of his conversion:

> As there was a great waking up among the churches from the revival that had broken out, many flocked to [such meetings]. The church would not hold the tenth part of the congregation. Accordingly the officers of the church erected a stand in a contiguous shady grove and prepared seats for a large congregation.
>
> The people crowded to this meeting from far and near. They came in their large wagons, with victuals mostly prepared. The women slept in the wagons, and the men under them. Many stayed on the ground night and day for a number of nights and days together. Others were provided for among the neighbors around. The power of God was wonderfully displayed; scores of sinners fell under the preaching, like men slain in mighty battle; Christians shouted aloud for joy.
>
> To this meeting I repaired—a guilty, wretched sinner. On the Saturday evening, I went with weeping multi-

tudes and bowed before the stand and earnestly prayed for mercy. In the midst of a solemn struggle of soul, an impression was made on my mind, as though a voice said to me, "Thy sins are all forgiven thee." Divine light flashed all round me, unspeakable joy sprung up in my soul.

I rose to my feet, opened my eyes, and it really seemed as if I was in heaven—the trees, the leaves on them, and everything, I really thought, were praising God. My mother raised the shout, my Christian friends crowded around me and joined me in praising God. And though I have been since then, in many instances, unfaithful, yet I have never, for one moment, doubted that the Lord did, then and there, forgive my sins and give me religion.[2]

Practical Deists

Many traditionalists discount any report of the supernatural. They question any message of divine healing. Miracles are suspect with them. Most traditionalists are practical deists. They say they believe in the reality of miracles, but they don't expect them.

David McKenna tells of an interesting encounter that should be helpful:

On a college campus recently a student leader responded enthusiastically to my lecture entitled "Welcome to the Awakening" by reporting how he had been baptized by the Holy Spirit, spoken in tongues and cast out demons. Reactive hairs on the back of my neck stood straight up. As an adult who had been readied in the Holiness tradition without tongues and as a psychologist who had defined demons in terms of psychosis, my first impulse was to reject the authenticity of his experience.

But then I choked on my own words. In the chapel address I had urged the students to be open to the stirrings of the Spirit, however they may come and wherever they may be. Who then was I to deny the unusual manifestation of the Spirit in this young man? So I shifted from negative body language to a positive reinforcement of his experience, though I urged him to undergird his leadership with serious study of the Word of God and the disciplines of his field of study.[3]

The Gift of Tongues as a Stumbling Block

The gifts of the Spirit usually make the traditionalists very nervous. It seems strange and foreign to their experience. They are afraid the practice may split the church. Charismatics should be sensitive to the feelings of the traditionalists and not push the promotion of gifts in the worship services. Traditionalists should recognize that the gifts of the Spirit are scriptural and not oppose those who have received them.

A major difference between Charismatics and Pentecostals is that Charismatics generally do not teach that the gift of tongues is necessary evidence of the baptism of the Holy Spirit.

Reconciliation of the Charismatics and Traditionalists

The traditionalists have stability. You can usually count on them in the good times and the bad. They have made many sacrifices in support of the church. We must not question their faith because they are more reserved and don't express their faith as you do. Many of them came to Christ at a different time and culture.

Charismatics can learn from the traditionalists. They have a loyalty that should be emulated. Also, they have an appreciation for tradition that enriches them. Traditionalists have love and respect for their denomination and recognize the great impact it has had for the kingdom of God and the potential it has for the future. They do not rely on feelings but often have deeply held convictions. Most don't go from church to church looking for a new "high" but remain faithful to their local congregation. They are likely to have respect for their pastor.

Charismatics are usually witnessing Christians. They have a zeal for the kingdom that is to be respected. Their joy seems to be overflowing. Indeed, their faith is contagious.

It seems to me that the faith and experience of the Charismatic and the traditionalist are complementary. They need each other and need to be tolerant of their differences. Together, they can make a great impact on the world and lead the way in the next Great Awakening.

Notes

1 *Encounter*, Vol. 29 (Winter 1967): 81.

2 *Christian History*, Issue 45, "Wrestling with God and Man," pp. 19–20.

3 David L McKenna, *The Coming Great Awakening* (Downers Grove, Ill.: Inter-Varsity Press, 1990), p. 64.

CHAPTER 11

New Wine in Old Wineskins

Can the Mainline Churches Be Part of a Holy Spirit Revival?

I have contended in this book that there is a great movement of the Holy Spirit taking place in the world today. It seems to me that any objective person will recognize this. The question is: Will the mainline churches be involved in this renewal? How great it would be if the historic churches would experience revival! They still have tremendous influence and power. Many members of Congress come from these churches. A larger percentage of the population belong to them. They have vast wealth and impressive institutions (hospitals, schools, etc.).

My own denomination, United Methodist, is a truly national church with a strong presence in every state. These churches could be a dynamic instrument for revival.

Independent churches have their faults and limitations. Sometimes there is a lack of accountability. Too often, they are built on a personality cult. When the minister gets into trouble the church fades.

There is usually a lack of balance. In a pluralistic church where everyone does not necessarily agree the message is likely to be more thoughtful.

In the major denominations there is organizational structure to deal with problems. When there is moral failure discipline can be exercised. Excesses can be constrained. There is a theological tradition that aids in the interpretation of Scripture and the Christian life.

The Holy Spirit is moving in power in many mainline congregations. Most of them have similar characteristics:

- They do not stress denominational affiliation.
- Most are flexible in structure.
- Worship is not highly liturgical, and they often combine the contemporary with the traditional.
- There is strong lay leadership.
- Evangelism and missions are a top priority.
- The Scriptures are reverenced as the written Word of God.
- Preaching is central to worship.
- They are not embarrassed by the supernatural but emphasize the ministry of the Holy Spirit.

One mainline church that is experiencing Charismatic renewal is the First United Methodist Church in Tulsa, Oklahoma. That congregation was a typical dead downtown church, declining in membership and vitality. Under the leadership of Dr. L. D. Thomas the congregation became open to the Holy Spirit. The fullness of the Spirit with accompanying gifts was experienced and celebrated. Traditionalists and Charismatics worshiped together, and they affirmed each other.

Now, under the leadership of Dr. Jimmy Buskirk, the church has continued to prosper. They now have more than 8,000 members and an average Sunday school attendance of over 2,200—with more than 1,000 of these being adults!

The church has just completed a $5,200,000 family life center. They have three morning worship services, with one being contemporary in style. On Saturday evenings they feature a Charismatic service where the gifts are expressed and often healings take place.

The church receives, on average, 450 new members each year. Additionally, they are a great missionary church, supporting 23 missionaries. Eighteen persons minister at First Church in a professional capacity.

This is one dynamic example of what can happen in mainline churches when the Holy Spirit is allowed to operate. There are many less dramatic illustrations of what is taking place in some United Methodist churches, and I rejoice equally in these less spectacular successes.

While we are rejoicing that some mainline churches are experiencing renewal we fully recognize that most are not. In fact, many actively resist the actions that would possibly lead to new life. Declining churches are also likely to have similar characteristics.

- They insist on classical music.
- Many frown on any display of emotion.
- Liberal theology that discounts the supernatural prevails.
- There is hostility toward the Charismatic movement.
- The authority of Scripture as the written Word of God is questioned.
- Evangelism is frowned upon and missions de-emphasized.
- Creative change is resisted vigorously.
- Personal salvation is not taught or proclaimed.

There are some that recognize the desperate situation of the traditional churches but their solution is to do what they have been doing, just do it better. That won't do. The crisis demands radical surgery, drastic change.

According to Andy Langford and Will Willimon:

The United Methodist Church faces a crisis unequaled to any since the schism preceding the Civil War. The continued membership decline is the major symptom of this crisis, but the issues are deeper and more complex than the loss of members. In any organization, when things are not going well, there are always those who urge silence, unquestioning loyalty, and the suppression of all criticism. But our church is too important to be allowed to wither.[1]

Many believe that the mainline churches are beyond reform and renewal. They remind us of the analogy of "new wine into old wineskins" used by Jesus in Matthew 9:17. Many of my friends point out that the Protestant Reformation and the Wesleyan revival required new structures. They contend that the old structures (denominations) are inflexible and too resistant to change.

Other friends contend that God has renewed his church many times. They point to the Anglican and Roman churches as examples. Richard Lovelace has written that established churches have been renewed frequently throughout history. He points to the Franciscan Order and the Counter Reformation as examples in the Roman Catholic Church.[2]

However, the barriers to renewal are formidable.

Cultural Barriers to Renewal

Persons over 60, who now make up the majority in many mainline churches, were reared in a different era. Their faith was formed when liberal theology was dominant and almost unchallenged. Most did not realize the subtle implications of this understanding of the faith. Church music was classical and the hymns were mostly written in the eighteenth and nineteenth centuries. Personal faith and salvation were not emphasized, and there was a reserve in speaking about one's relationship to God. They feel uncomfortable with scriptural choruses and persons raising their hands in praise to God. Any spontaneous expression of faith in worship is criticized. Many yearn for a past that is fading away and is not likely to return. That generation is more loyal to the institution and proud of their denominational affiliation.

I grew up in that culture. I am very comfortable with traditional worship. When I was a young man, practically all Methodist churches used the *Gloria Patri,* Doxology, responsive readings, and the Apostles' Creed. The divided chancel was the exception, not the rule. Very few ministers wore robes. Choirs would sing classical anthems and the congregational hymns were written in the eighteenth and nineteenth centuries.

Most churches had Sunday evening services, and the singing would be revival-type songs, generally from the *Cokesbury Hymnal.* Attendance was usually good, budgets were growing, and new church buildings were being erected. Youth groups were learning to folk dance, and youth camps were expanding. We didn't know we were going on the momentum of the past.

As I said earlier, it takes three generations to backslide. The first generation has the experiences and commitment. The second generation has the memory and respect. But the third generation has lost the memory and respect. I suspect that I was a contemporary of the second generation. We are now seeing the fruit of the third generation.

Organizational Barriers to Renewal

It is in the vested interest of the ecclesiastical leadership to maintain the status quo. They owe their positions of privilege and power to the present system. They feel threatened by dynamic unofficial programs such as Promise Keepers. Initiative is encouraged from the top down rather than from the local church up.

The power of pastoral appointments inhibits pastors from being prophetic and bold. Too often, they are discouraged from pursuing creative programs and contemporary worship styles. The financial resources required to maintain a vast, faceless bureaucracy is crippling the local church. The itinerate ministry with relatively short pastoral appointments discourages them from developing their own ethos and ensures greater control by the hierarchy. Conformity is encouraged and individual initiative may be considered disloyal.

Theological Barriers to Renewal

The Holy Spirit cannot bless heresy.

Churches that question the authority of Scripture as the written Word of God will not experience renewal. As the Apostle Paul writes, "if the trumpet does not sound a clear call, who will get ready for battle?" (1 Corinthians 14:8).

The church that denies the centrality of Christ will not be blessed with vitality and growth. Dynamic churches will "offer them Christ." They are convinced of the uniqueness of Jesus. As Dr. Albert Outler so well said:

A Christian theologian need not apologize for talking about Jesus Christ for, as a matter of fact, he hasn't anything else *really distinctive* to talk about. Christianity shares much else with the other religions and philosophies of life—but not Jesus Christ.[3]

Vital churches faithfully remember the words of our Lord, "I am the way and the truth and the life. No one comes to the Father except through me" (John 14:6). And they remember the witness of Peter when he said, ". . . for there is no other name under heaven given to men by which we must be saved" (Acts 4:12).

Universalism has crept into many of the historic churches. This is the doctrine that teaches all will finally be saved regardless of lifestyle or faith. Also, some are now advocating syncretism, the heresy that believes there is truth in all religions and rather than converting persons of other faiths, we should affirm them and celebrate our differences.

Ichabod! The glory has departed from churches that teach this kind of radical theology.

Lifestyle Barriers to Renewal

The greatest barrier to renewal in the church is a lack of commitment. A "laid back" type of faith is not likely to be blessed by the Lord. Our highest priority must be the Christian faith with all its implications. Discipleship must be taken seriously. An indulgent, soft, undisciplined lifestyle will not be blessed of God. Materialism is seldom mentioned in evangelical, Charismatic or liberal churches. The values of Christians do not seem to be greatly different from those of the secularists.

Churches of every theological persuasion are plagued with materialism. Revival will not likely come to a worldly church. The symbol of the Christian faith is the cross, a sign of suffering, sacrifice and death, not dollar signs.

I believe the mainline churches with their vast resources and high membership are worth saving. The question is "how?"

The Barrier of Dead Orthodoxy

A lifeless, dead orthodoxy is a stench in the nostrils of God. A narrow fundamentalism without the power of the Holy Spirit is unattractive and rigid. These types of churches are often guilty of "bibliolatry," that is, the worship of the Bible rather than the Lord of the Bible. They are not open to fresh expressions of the Holy Spirit and new insights. Too often, they are legalists that believe the right things but do not have the freedom and joy of the Spirit-filled life.

I believe in a sovereign God who is able to do more than we can ask or think. A mighty Holy Ghost revival can sweep away the barriers. As Wesleyan Christians we need to reclaim our heritage of experiential religion with biblical authority. We must bombard heaven with our prayers, claiming our churches for Christ.

Strategy for Renewal

What should be the strategy for seeking renewal in the main-line denominations?

First of all, we need to remember we cannot program the Holy Spirit. He is sovereign and moves where he desires. It may be that it is not in his plan to renew the historic churches. They may continue to decline and the future may be with the independent, Charismatic and Pentecostal churches. However, I am not willing to concede this. I believe that if we will pay the price in prayer and commitment God will send a mighty revival.

There are many at the grass roots who have had a Charismatic experience. According to one recent George Barna poll, seven percent of all American Christians profess to receiving the gift of tongues.[4]

More than 2,500 Charismatic United Methodists attended a recent conference on the working of the Holy Spirit. Participants from across the United States, Russia and the Philippines attended Aldersgate '96, the eighteenth conference on the Holy Spirit. This annual event is the United Methodist version of the Charismatic movement that has swept through mainline Protestant denominations for more than 30 years.

The conferences are the annual gatherings of people involved in Aldersgate Renewal Ministries, the working name of the United Methodist Renewal Services Fellowship, Inc. This is a network of United Methodists who pray and work together for the denomination's spiritual renewal through the power of the Holy Spirit.

Many of these good Spirit-filled people will go elsewhere if they are not affirmed and encouraged to express their faith. Do you remember the United Methodist evangelist Mark Rutland, whom I mentioned in an earlier chapter? His inspiring ministry was having a very positive impact upon United Methodist churches in his native South and nationwide. Yet, sadly, he eventually felt alienated from the denomination and decided to join the Assemblies of God. They welcomed him. We cannot afford many losses like this.

I would advocate asking denominational leaders (bishops and district superintendents) to appoint Charismatic pastors to declining churches in transitional neighborhoods and give them the freedom to have contemporary worship services and to celebrate the gifts of the Spirit. A traditional type ministry will not survive in blue-collar communities. Charismatic worship will reach persons from different ethnic groups and the economically deprived. That is really the only way these marginal churches will survive.

In every town of 15,000 or more there is room for more than one United Methodist church, especially in growing areas. Why not establish a new congregation for those who desire a church that unapologetically celebrates the Spirit-filled life? This could reverse the decline in membership and positively impact the denomination. These churches would not be viewed as second-class stepchildren but full partners in a pluralistic church.

In churches all across America there are prayer and Bible study groups that encourage and inspire. These groups are usually made up of committed Christians. Zeal and joy are contagious. If these persons will remain humble and do not imply spiritual superiority, they can influence a congregation to be open to the Holy Spirit.

God is sovereign but he usually responds to his children's prayers. The Christian's secret weapon is prayer. We read in 2 Chronicles 7:14, "if my people, who are called by my name, will humble themselves and pray and seek my face and turn from their wicked ways, then will I hear from heaven and will forgive their sin and will heal their land."

So, can "new wine" be poured successfully into "old wine-skins"? I believe the answer to be yes, *if* the old wineskins—we ourselves—are willing to be changed and renewed by the power of the Spirit. We can only contain today's spiritual blessings if we are willing to be remade by God in our day. Are we willing?

Let us seek the face of God, get hold of the horns of the altar and cry out, "I will not let you go until you bless me."

Notes

1 Andy Langford and William H. Willimon, *A New Connection: Reforming The United Methodist Church* (Nashville: Abingdon Press, 1995), p. 13.

2 Richard F. Lovelace, *Dynamics of Spiritual Life: An Evangelical Theology of Renewal* (Downers Grove, IL: Inter-Varsity Press, 1979), pp. 33–34.

3 Albert Outler, *Christology*, ed., Tom Oden (Anderson, Ind.: Bristol Books, 1996), p. 19.

4 "Barna's Polls on Religion," *The Washington Times*, August 25, 1996.

CHAPTER 12

The Next Great Awakening

Is It Coming? How Will It Come?

*A*n English bishop visited America in the early colonial period. When he returned home he said that with the death of the older families the church would be gone in America. Only about five percent of the population were church members. The future looked bleak.

But out of the wilderness came a prophetic voice. The Reverend Jonathan Edwards, a Puritan preacher in the tradition of John the Baptist, put out a call to personal repentance. Edward's sermon, "Sinners in the Hands of an Angry God," preached at Enfield, Connecticut, in 1741, was the turning point in the history of Great Awakenings.

Revival followed, not just on the confession of sin, but also the promise of joy that Edwards preached. He reported hundreds of conversions sealed by public confession among the churches of New England.[1]

The Awakening spread under the impetus of a twenty-three year old itinerant preacher from England named George

Whitefield. Fresh from the experience of the Evangelical Awakening in England where he convinced John Wesley to take to the open fields for his preaching, Whitefield traveled to the colonies—against the opposition of the Anglican clergy—to take the gospel to the unchurched.[2]

The first Great Awakening changed the course of American history. David McKenna has written, "American history can be written through its Great Awakenings."[3]

The inception of the Second Great Awakening in America can be dated from 1795. Religion was in decline following the Revolutionary War. Into this climate of corruption God called Timothy Dwight, grandson of Jonathan Edwards, to be president of Yale in 1795. Fearlessly, Dwight chose his first sermon to invite all students to an open forum on the Christian faith. After hearing their attacks, he followed with a chapel series in which he spoke the "truth with love"—so much so that one-half of the student body professed Christ before the year was out. One by one, spontaneous stirring took place on college campuses.[4]

In 1808, five young men, students at Williams College, took refuge under a haystack during a rainstorm. They had a prayer meeting under that haystack and were led by the Holy Spirit to organize "The Society of Brethren." It was a secret missionary organization. This was the beginning of the modern missionary movement in America which was one of the fruits of the Second Great Awakening.[5]

The western frontier was challenged and conquered during the Second Great Awakening. Peter Cartwright was an example of the rugged Methodist preacher who was mightily used of the Lord to tame and evangelize the wild frontier.

Here is an account of one of his services:

> While I was preaching, near the close of the discourse, suddenly the power of God fell on the congregation like a flash of lightning, and the people fell right and left;

some screamed aloud for mercy, others fell on their knees and prayed aloud . . . About 12 were converted in the good old way, and shouted aloud the praises of God.[6]

On another occasion Cartwright wrote:

I was just closing my sermon, and pressing it with all the force I could command, when the power of God was suddenly displayed, and sinners fell by the scores through the assembly. We had no need of a mourners' bench. It was supposed that several hundred fell in five minutes; sinners turned pale; some ran into the woods, and tried to get away and fell in the attempt, and some shouted for joy.[7]

Concerning the preparations of preachers Peter Cartwright wrote:

I do believe that if ministers of the present day had more of the unction or baptized fire of the Holy Ghost prompting their ministerial efforts, we should succeed much better than we do, and be more successful in winning souls to Christ than we are. If those ministers, or young men that think they are called of God to minister in the word and doctrines of Jesus Christ, were to cultivate a holy life, a better knowledge of this supreme agency of the Divine Spirit, and depend less on the learned theological knowledge of biblical institutes, it is my opinion they would do vastly more good than they are likely to do . . . Is this not the grand secret of the success of the early pioneer preachers, from John Wesley down to the present day?[8]

Cartwright described the early Methodist preacher this way:

A Methodist preacher in those days, when he felt that God had called him to preach, instead of hunting up a college or biblical institute, hunted a hearty pony or horse, and some traveling apparatus, and with his library always at hand, namely, Bible, hymn book, and Discipline, he started with a text that never wore out or grew stale. He cried, "Behold, the Lamb of God that taketh away the sin of the world." In this way, he went through storms of wind, hail, snow, and rain; climbed hills, and mountains, traversed valleys, plunged through swamps, swam swollen streams, lay out all night, wet, weary, and hungry, held his horse by the bridle all night or tied him to a limb, slept with his saddle blanket for a bed, his saddle or saddle bags for his pillow and his old coat or blanket if he had any, for a covering. Often he slept in dirty cabins, on earthen floors, before the fire: ate roasting ears for bread, drank buttermilk for coffee, or sage tea for imperial: took with hardy zest deer or bear meat, or wild turkey, for breakfast, dinner and supper, if he could get it. His text was always ready, "Behold, the Lamb of God." This was the old-fashion Methodist preacher's fare and fortune. Under such circumstance, who among us would now say, "Here am I Lord, send me"?[9]

Such were the men that conquered the frontier.

Not all awakenings have been so distant or well defined as the First and Second Great Awakenings, but throughout American history periodically there have been unusual movements of the Holy Spirit.

In 1886, evangelist Dwight L. Moody called an epoch-making student conference at Mount Hermon. It was called "The Meeting of the Ten Nations." Moody declared, "The world has not seen what God can do through a young man thoroughly consecrated." Robert Wilder, son of Royal Wilder of the Haystack Band, challenged the students with the exhortation, "Ask not why we should go, but why we should not go." The

Princeton Volunteers coined the phrase that was to become the students' watchword, "The evangelization of the World in this generation."[10]

Toward the end of the nineteenth century, there was a significant movement of the Holy Spirit in America and England.

• • •

Historically, revivals have often started on college campuses. Young people have led the way under the blessing and leadership of the Holy Spirit.

The Holy Club at Oxford University under the leadership of the Wesleys was a unique instrument of God as a catalyst for the Evangelical Awakening in England. The participants were all young persons.

Yale College under the preaching of President Timothy Dwight was perhaps the first spark of the Second Great Awakening.

The Society of Brethren, mentioned earlier, was the beginning of the modern missionary movement in America. It started at Williams College in 1808 following the famous "haystack prayer meeting." The movement quickly spread to other campuses. The Second Great Awakening continued to spread throughout America and the world.

The student conference in 1886 called "The Meeting of the Ten Nations" led by evangelist Dwight L. Moody is another example of youth movements being mightily used of the Holy Spirit to bring revival. In the years following this conference more than 10,000 missionaries went to the ends of the earth as missionaries of Jesus Christ.

In the twentieth century we have witnessed many great spontaneous campus revivals. Perhaps the best known college revival was the Asbury revival of 1970. The fire fell in a chapel service on February 3. It was a time of confession and praise. Classes were suspended for a week. Seekers were at the altar

day and night. The hymn that became the theme of this sponta-
neous movement of the Holy Spirit was, "There's a Sweet, Sweet
Spirit in This Place." The revival spread to campuses all over
America. Many were swept into the kingdom and to a Spirit-
filled life as a result of this marvelous movement of the Holy
Spirit.

A spontaneous revival of the Holy Spirit broke out in the
West Central Texas college town of Brownwood in 1995, and
has been spreading from college campus to college campus ever
since.[11]

Centered at the Coggin Avenue Baptist Church, which is the
campus church to the Baptist-affiliated Howard Payne College
in Brownwood, the revival broke out suddenly during Sunday
services in January.

People suddenly began confessing their sins, seeking God,
and praying for forgiveness. A hardened ranch hand listening to
the service on his truck radio was converted. A prominent local
business man who had been considering suicide was transformed.
Couples just days from divorce confessed and were restored.

Within hours, the movement had spread to Howard Payne
campus. Students lined up at microphones to confess their sins,
in scenes reminiscent of the great Asbury College revival of 1970.

One of the most amazing aspects of the Brownwood revival
is that Baptists have begun cooperating with Pentecostal, Charismatic, Nazarene and other congregations. One project the
churches are working on together is reaching youth gang members for Christ. Many young people have been converted as a
result.

From Howard Payne, the revival has spread to Wheaton
College, Trinity Seminary, Asbury College, Gordon College, and
many others.[12] Everywhere the emphasis is the same—repentance!

Hopefully, the youth of the church will lead us in the next
Great Awakening.

As I finish work on this manuscript, we have just heard the jury's verdict on the O. J. Simpson civil trial. The dramatic news coverage of this trial, and that of Simpson's criminal trial, has polarized American public opinion. African Americans generally believe Simpson to be innocent while the great majority of whites are convinced that he is guilty. There is a deep division in this country that seems to be growing. Many thoughtful people are fearful for the future of this nation with racism and hatred so evident. The breakdown of the family and soured race relations are the greatest social problems in this country.

Does the Church Have the Answer?

Conventional religion in its liberal expression stands impotent before the great social problems of our society.

Harvey Cox in his book, *Fire from Heaven*, illustrates this difference between mainline religion and the Pentecostal revival of the twentieth century with the following illustration.

Among the many configurations of the future to appear at the turn of the last century, two stood out. One was the great Columbian Exposition, which drew millions of people to Chicago in the summer of 1893. It was the inspired creation of a company of gifted architects, canny financiers, and cosmopolitan religious leaders. The second, according to Cox, was the lesser known Azusa Street revival that took place a decade later in Los Angeles around a cluster of down-at-the-heels hymn singers and itinerant evangelists, which marked the birth of the worldwide Pentecostal movement.[13]

The Exposition was planned to celebrate the four hundredth anniversary of Christopher Columbus' discovery of America. The planners dubbed it the "White City" because of the plaster material that encased the iron frames. It glistened with lustrous sheen. Some called it the "New Jerusalem."

One of the principal events that took place at the Exposition was "The Parliament of Religions." It was the first attempt in

history to assemble representatives of all the major faiths in order to seek a common spiritual basis for global unity. The meetings lasted 17 days, and thousands of enthusiastic guests lined
up every morning to attend the open sessions.

One year later, the "White City" burned to the ground, completely destroyed. The sublime pavilions of the "New Jerusalem" were gone.

The World's Columbian Exposition held in 1893 was the
consummate symbol of America's pride in its brief past and confidence in its limitless future. To many, this outsized jamboree
became both a new Pentecost and a new Jerusalem rolled into
one.

The second turn-of-the-century harbinger was the Azusa
Street revival. The Pentecostal movement burst forth in 1906
amid unpromising circumstances in a run-down section of Los
Angeles. Led by an African-American preacher with no theological education, its first adherents were poor domestic servants, janitors, and day workers, black and white, who had the
audacity to claim that a new Pentecost was happening.[14]

The learned and accomplished delegates to the parliament
were drawn from the religious and educational elite. The Pentecostal movement, on the other hand, erupted from among
society's disenfranchised.

Today, the records of the Parliament of Religions molder on
library shelves. But the Pentecostal movement is thriving.[15]

Not a single one of the men and women who would soon
become the voices of the Pentecostal upsurge was present in
Chicago. They were not among the famous and the sought-after
who gathered under the spell of the White City. No one knew
their names. Today, however, Pentecostals number over
400,000,000 while few remember or care about the Parliament
of Religions.

The White City and the Parliament of Religions symbolize
liberal mainline Protestantism and its impotency in this neo-

pagan society. Earthly fires destroyed the White City. The heavenly fires of the Holy Spirit ignited the Pentecostal movement into a mighty movement for God.

When Will the Next Great Awakening Come?

A leading bishop said to me recently, "It seems to me that Satan has unleashed an unprecedented attack on the clergy." He was concerned with the many moral failures in the ministry. We have all read about high profile TV evangelists who have been involved in scandals. There have also been pastors of large mainline churches and even bishops who have been disgraced by moral failure. God cannot bless this kind of moral rot.

The great reformers and evangelists of the past great awakenings have been persons of impeccable integrity. There has not been even a hint of scandal with any of them. Ethical discipline must be restored to the church if we are going to experience revival. It is not without significance that the prevailing characteristic of the Brownwood revival is repentance.

The message of the Old Testament prophets was repentance (Ezekiel 14:6.) John the Baptist came preaching repentance, (Matthew 3:2). Jesus' message was, "Repent for the kingdom of heaven is near" (Matthew 4:17). The first gospel sermon was preached by Peter who said, "Repent and be baptized, every one of you, in the name of Jesus Christ so that your sins may be forgiven" (Acts 2:38).

The missing note of the current revival is "repentance." We are not going to have a Great Awakening until we hear a clear message and also experience repentance. A worldly church must take inventory and be honest. Repentance must begin at the house of God.

It was a sad day when tears left the church and went to the theater. May the Holy Spirit convict us of our coldness of heart, burden us for the sins of the world, and give us a concern for the lostness of humanity.

Awakenings usually do not come from the top down but rather they come from the bottom up. Almost all great movements of the Spirit have been initially opposed by the church hierarchy. Most of the revivalists have not been theologically trained. That includes Peter Cartwright, Charles Finney, Dwight L. Moody, Billy Sunday, Billy Graham and Oral Roberts. Some have not been ordained. Indeed, it is often laymen who have taken the leadership in renewal movements.

Fire from heaven descended on April 9, 1906, on a small band of black domestic servants, and custodial employees gathered for prayer in a wooden house on North Bonnie Brae Avenue in Los Angeles, California. Their leader, as discussed earlier, was a self-educated traveling preacher named William Joseph Seymour. He and his tiny company continued to meet in kitchens and parlors, praying that God would renew and purify a Christianity they believed was crippled by empty rituals, dried up creeds and the sin of racial bigotry.[16]

> When the fire finally fell, shouts of joy and rapturous dancing before the Spirit resounded throughout the neighborhood The word got out. Night after night, people crowded into that little house, stood on the porch, and stopped to listen and catch a glimpse. White people began to come, and Mexicans. Soon, the crowds grew too large, so Seymour and his friends rented a small abandoned church on nearby Azusa Street which had been used as a warehouse and a livery stable. . . .[17]

The Azusa Street revival continued day after day, month after month, for three years. The modern Pentecostal movement was born.

These great outpourings of the past are not the last Word from God. I am convinced that a great awakening of worldwide dimensions is about to occur.

What Are the Characteristics of This Third Great Awakening?

The Protestant Reformation theme was, "The just shall live by faith."

The emphases of the Evangelical revival in England under the Wesleys were assurance and holiness.

In the First Great Awakening led by Jonathan Edwards and George Whitefield, the prevailing message was the new birth.

In the Second Great Awakening the emphasis was on the implications of the gospel resulting in moral reformation and the birth of the modern missionary movement. The social gospel and the abolitionist movement were by-products of this revival.

The dominant message of the next great awakening will be the ministry of the Holy Spirit with the fruit and gifts experienced and celebrated. Supernatural manifestations will not be uncommon. Visions and prophecies will occur with increasing frequency. Evangelism will again become the primary task of the church. Churches that are open to the Holy Spirit will experience remarkable growth.

There will be a unity of believers in the next Great Awakening. It won't be an artificial structure from the top such as COCU[18] but will be a result of a common experience of the Holy Spirit and commitment to the Lord Jesus Christ. The importance of denominations will fade. Already, especially among young adults, we are seeing a decline in interest in and loyalty to denominations.

I have noticed when the Spirit is moving and manifesting himself in power, people don't care what the sectarian affiliation of others is. Structural union is usually the concern of declining churches. Unity comes among believers who are Spirit-filled. Many of the most dynamic renewal movements of our time are interdenominational. Local churches are looking for leadership from evangelical and Charismatic organizations outside the main denominational structures.

It has often been said that eleven o'clock on Sunday morning is the most segregated hour of the week. I am afraid this is true.

The mainline churches have responded to racial divisions with quotas and affirmative action in the church bureaucracy and appointing some black pastors to predominately white congregations. The church-at-large remains as segregated as ever. In fact, this has contributed to the leadership vacuum in African-American local churches. Many of the most talented ethnic preachers are given positions in the ecclesiastical hierarchy when they are desperately needed in the local churches.

In visiting Charismatic churches recently, I noticed a significant black presence: When I attend mainline traditional churches, I find they are lily-white. The liberals have been preaching racial justice from the safe distance of the suburbs while the Pentecostals have been ministering in the ghettos of the inner-city.

The style of worship of the Charismatics may be more compatible to many African Americans, but this is not the full explanation. The Holy Spirit breaks down the barriers and makes us one in Jesus Christ. The social activist looks to government programs for justice and equality and I am sure some of this is necessary. But government programs will never break down hatred, racism, anger and prejudice. This will come when we are a family—brothers and sisters in Christ. Personal relationships in the body of Christ can and will bring healing.

In the next great awakening Christians will be color-blind. We must be intentional in seeking to build relationships and working for a just society.

Conservative Christians too often in the past have been callous in their attitude toward ethnic persons. The liberals have convinced them that they are their friends, and perhaps they are. At least they have been sensitive to the needs and feelings of ethnic persons. But still the racial problems grow and polarization is a widening reality.

Enlightened Spirit-filled leadership will lead the way in building a reconciled community as the family of God. This will not happen because of human programs, as good and fine as they may be, but will be the result of Pentecost. Racism must go. We will either have the fires of God's judgment or the fire of the Holy Spirit.

The mainline churches have lost the ability to communicate or identify with the poor and uneducated. Traditional congregations consist primarily of middle-class people. They have crusaded for economic reform and supported the welfare state. Indeed, they have allied with labor unions, Ralph Nader and left-wing organizations seeking to help the poor and disinherited. I believe, for the most part, their concern is genuine. But often the poor—like people at all economic levels—are struggling with alcohol, drugs, sexual immorality, divorce, and illegitimacy. They desperately need personal salvation.

In the next great awakening evangelicals will have a renewed interest in the plight of the poor and will become their advocates. Also, Christians will learn to communicate with those who are educationally deprived and struggling with personal sins. We will identify with the poor and recognize that in the kingdom of God there are no classes but all are brothers and sisters in Christ.

Conclusion

I have one great overriding concern as I conclude this book. Will the traditional mainline churches be open to the next great awakening? Can we put new wine into old wineskins?

Will the mainline churches reject the radical liberalism that has almost destroyed them?

Will traditional churches insist on highly liturgical worship services that turn off the baby boomers and are rejected by the X generation?

How will most denominational churches react when the gifts of the Spirit are exercised in the congregation?

Will churches resist change and gradually die, or be open to the mighty movement of the Holy Spirit and live?

Notes

1 *The Coming Great Awakening,* David McKenna (Downers Grove, Ill.: Inter-Varsity Press, 1979) p. 30.

2 Ibid., p. 31.

3 Ibid., p. 30.

4 Ibid., p. 34.

5 Edmund W. Robb, *The World Forever Our Parish,* Dean S. Gilliland, ed. (Anderson, Ind.: Bristol Books, 1991), p. 115.

6 *Autobiography of Peter Cartwright* (1856, reprint. Nashville: Abingdon Press, reprinted 1956) p. 88.

7 Ibid., p. 89.

8 Ibid., p. 144.

9 Ibid., p. 164.

10 *Alert!* (a newsletter of the Ed Robb Evangelistic Association, Marshall, Texas), Vol. 1, p. 1, October, 1995.

11 John Avant, *Challenge to Evangelism Today,* Spring, 1996, p. 7.

12 Ibid., p. 1.

13 Harvey Cox, *Fire From Heaven,* p. 24.

14 Ibid., p. 41.

15 Ibid., p. 46.

16 Ibid.

17 Ibid.

18 Consultation on Church Union.

CHAPTER 13

The Conclusion—Living the Spirit-Filled Life

A Summary of My Beliefs about the Holy Spirit

*J*n this book I have covered a lot of ground, involving church history, Wesleyan theology, how the Spirit operates, the ins and outs of the new Holy Spirit movements, and more. Perhaps I have covered too much ground.

This last chapter is taken from the sermon on the Holy Spirit I have given throughout the United States. Everywhere I go to preach the most requested subject is the Spirit. People are hungry for knowledge of how God's Spirit can become real in their lives. Some readers may profit from the following pages, which fairly summarize my beliefs concerning and experience with the Holy Spirit

Our Need for Holiness

Humanity has two great spiritual needs—the first one is forgiveness. God met that need at Calvary. The second great need is holiness and God met that need at Pentecost.[1] The first, in the cross, is God's work for us. The second, the Holy Spirit at Pentecost, is God's work in us. We need Jesus Christ for our eternal life but we need the Holy Spirit for our internal life. Jesus Christ takes us to heaven. The Holy Spirit brings something of heaven to us in the here and now. We are no longer living in the days of promise. These are the days of fulfillment. Before Pentecost the emphasis was on the word *ask*. After Pentecost the emphasis was on the word *receive*.[2]

Many people are confused and say they don't understand the Holy Spirit.

Remember this—*There is nothing that God is that the Holy Spirit is not.* As Christians we pray to the Father, through the Son, in the Spirit. We believe in the Holy Trinity. Some say they don't understand this business of one God and three personalities. The Trinity is a mystery. Perhaps this will help them. The Trinity is not one plus one plus one equals three, but the Trinity is one times one times one equals one. We sing, "God in three persons, blessed Trinity."[3]

A New Pentecost

I believe we need a new Pentecost. Every Christian has been to Calvary but every Christian has not yet experienced Pentecost. Every redeemed person has been to the cross and every victorious Christian has been filled with the Holy Spirit. Pentecost was a divine breakthrough. It was greatly needed in the days of the apostles just as a new divine breakthrough is desperately needed in our time. We can't be the church that God called us to be in our own strength and by our own wisdom. We can't be the persons, the Christians, that God intends for us to be in our own strength. Many of us have been trying to live the Christian life in our own strength but we need the "divine plus" to enable us to be the kind of persons that we want to be.

The Holy Spirit brought to life a group of believers and made them in fact the body of Christ. It is by the power of the Holy

Spirit that the church is more than an organization. By the Holy Spirit the church becomes an organism—alive, vital. This is what makes the church unique among all the institutions of the world. "Christ in you the hope of glory." Before Pentecost, religion is doctrine and rules—sometimes dead doctrine and harsh rules. That's not very attractive. I am sometimes afraid persons get the idea that Christianity is a set of rules. They say, "Don't do this; you shouldn't do that; you ought to be doing better; you ought to do this." After Pentecost, Christianity is life and power.

The first Pentecost was an Old Testament festival. It was celebrated in commemoration of Moses' receiving the law on Mt. Sinai. So, on the first Pentecost the law was written on tablets of stone— but at the second Pentecost with the coming of the Holy Spirit, the law was written on the fleshly tablets of the heart. True religion was changed from legalism to freedom— from the negative to the positive. Most persons are open to that kind of religion.

The Holy Spirit came at Pentecost. Dr. J. D. Jones wrote these words, "Easter gave to the church its gospel, Pentecost gave to the church its power." Dr. Paul S. Rees, the prince of preachers of our time, wrote these words, "Easter is Christ risen on behalf of his church, Pentecost is Christ released within the very heart of his church."

Cardinal Leon Suenens was the head of the renewal movement in the Roman Catholic Church. It is wonderful what is happening in some areas of the Roman Catholic Church—unusual, unexpected things are taking place in some areas of that historic church.

Sometime ago I was in New York City. Two other preachers and I caught a cab. The taxi driver was a woman. She was saying, "Hallelujah, glory, praise the Lord." I thought, well, we have a Pentecostal cab driver. After a bit I said, "What church do you belong to?" She said, "I am a Roman Catholic and we are going to Rome this summer to witness to the Holy Father." I thought, "My, this is a new day."

A Foundation for Theological Education (AFTE) had a colloquy at Notre Dame University several years ago. One of the speakers was to be Cardinal Leon Suenens but the Pope called a consistory in Rome. So he sent his colleague to read his paper. He gave one of the greatest testimonies of the power of Christ that I've ever heard. This is a quote from his paper: "If there is a major problem in the church today it is that we don't believe enough in the presence of the Holy Spirit in our lives." I think the Cardinal was exactly right.

Pentecost was a harvest festival celebrated in the Old Testament period. It was a time of rejoicing, of thanksgiving, and of praise. My wife and I were on the island of Java. It was Pentecost Sunday. We were in Jakarta, and I was invited to preach at the Chinese Presbyterian Church. I learned that they had their morning service at sunrise. Jakarta is on the equator and twelve months out of the year sunrise is at 6:00 a.m. The church was packed. As I approached the door the head elder was standing there. He took me into a side room to pray with the elders. They put their hands upon my Bible and prayed that the Holy Spirit would bless the word that was to be proclaimed that day. We went in the sanctuary where they had a high pulpit with ascending stairs. When it came time for me to preach I approached the stairs and the elder handed me my Bible. I preached the unsearchable riches of Jesus through an interpreter.

As I descended the pulpit stairs the elder was there. He took my Bible. Again we went into a side room and they prayed the Holy Spirit would bless the Word that had been proclaimed. That emphasized to me the connection between God's Word and the Holy Spirit. It's the Holy Spirit that makes the Bible come alive. It's the Holy Spirit that is the best interpreter for this book.

Later that day, I was to preach for the Javanese Reformed Church at 11:00 o'clock. That's the time that God speaks to us in Texas. I went into that sanctuary and there was a sight to behold. All across the front there was exotic fruit and tropical produce—pineapple, bananas, tapioca, tea. I thought, "Pentecost, a time of harvest and how appropriate it is." Then I thought, "We are not going to have a spiritual harvest, we are not going to see a harvest of souls until we have a new Pentecost, until we have a fresh outpouring of the Holy Spirit."

The Church's Need Today

Admiration for the men and women through whom the Holy Spirit worked so mightily in the book of Acts needs to be followed with appropriation of that self-same Spirit for a miracle today. As United Methodists we are great at talking about Wesley, but I ask, "Where is the God of Wesley?"

We talk about Francis Asbury, the prophet of the long trail, and how he established Methodism in this land. I ask, "Where is the God of Francis Asbury?" We talk about the circuit riders, how they carved out of this wilderness a great civilization in the name of God. I tell you it's time for the church to stop retreating. For the God that blessed Wesley will bless us. The God who used Francis Asbury is the God who will use us. The God who blessed those circuit riders with so many converts and made them instruments for revival is the God who will use us today. We need to do more than celebrate Pentecost season, we need a new Pentecost. We need to do more than remember Aldersgate Sunday, we need the experience of the warm heart.

A Fresh Outpouring of the Holy Spirit

We need a fresh outpouring of the Holy Spirit.

Samuel Shoemaker is one of my heroes. Sometime ago I read his biography. He left a life of privilege to enter the priesthood of the Episcopal Church. He was a spiritual father of Alcoholics Anonymous. He organized "Faith at Work." At the end of his life, he died a relatively young man, his wife sitting at his bedside. He looked up at her and said, "Sweetheart, it's been a good run."[4]

I thought, when you run with Jesus in the power of the Spirit, whether the life is short or whether the life is long, you will always be able to say, "It's been a good run." When I read that I thought about W. E. Sangster, who pastored the largest Methodist congregation in all of England. He also died a relatively young man.

On the last Easter of his life his family was at church, his daughter was at his bedside. He could not walk, he could not talk. He could only write with great effort. He indicated to his daughter that he wanted a pencil. This is what he wrote: "Easter, and what a tragedy—no tongue to proclaim the risen Christ. I can think of but one greater tragedy and that is to have a tongue and no risen Christ to proclaim."[5]

When I was in London, I stood in Westminster Hall in Sangster's old pulpit, and I prayed that the spirit of Sangster would come upon me because that was the Holy Spirit.

Samuel Shoemaker said, "We need to step from the marginal waters of the Christian experience into the stream of the Spirit." Did you ever go swimming a little early in the spring and the water was cold and you'd put your toe in and you'd pull it back, you'd put your foot in and you'd pull it back. There is just one thing to do in that situation, and that is to jump in.

So it is with many of us. We have been testing the spiritual waters. We're interested. We put our toe in, and we pull back. But friends, "Let go and let God." I know why you don't. You are afraid you will lose control, but haven't you already made a big enough mess of your life being in control yourself? Don't you need to let the Holy Spirit take over in your life?

One day while my son Ed was in seminary we were talking about the Holy Spirit. He said, "Dad, I don't like the term Spirit-filled." That upset me. I said, "Why not?" He said, "I prefer the term Spirit-controlled." I said, "Ed, to be Spirit-filled is to be Spirit-controlled." We need to get in the stream of the Spirit.

What Happened on the Day of Pentecost?

What happened on the day of Pentecost and afterward? The first thing I noticed was these disciples were transformed. Cowards became courageous, the timid became bold, the sinful became righteous. This is always the first evidence of a Spirit-filled life. Persons are transformed. You and I can be transformed when the Spirit of God takes control of our lives.

There were Jews present from all over the Roman Empire to celebrate Pentecost. When Peter preached, they understood him. This evidently was not glossolalia. Some scholars believe this is what happened. All good Jewish boys were sent to the synagogue school to learn Hebrew. But the Jewish boys who grew up in Rome and Greece and Egypt soon lost the ability to speak Hebrew.

Some believe that the Holy Spirit enabled Peter to preach in Hebrew and that the congregation—the Jews from all over the Roman Empire—understood. The greater miracle is that when the Holy Spirit comes the barriers are broken down. The barriers of denomination are broken down, the barriers of generations are broken down, the barriers of race are broken down and we are enabled to communicate and be one in Jesus Christ.

There were those who received gifts of the Holy Spirit. The gift of healing, the gift of prophecy, the gift of discernment, the gift of administration, the gift of tongues, and the gift of interpretation of tongues. Now you say, "I don't understand all of that." Well, I don't either. But, I am convinced that the gifts of the Spirit are operative in the church today. But as I read in 1 Corinthians 12 I find that not any single gift is a necessary evidence of the Spirit-filled life.

I may have the gift of administration. Others may have the gift of discernment. Someone else may have the gift of prophecy and that could be interpreted as a gift for preaching. Let us not ever base our fellowship on whether a person has a particular gift.

The Bible does not say, "by their gifts you will recognize them." What it does say is, "by their fruit you will recognize them" (Matthew 7:16). So we should seek the fullness of the Holy Spirit in our lives and praise God for any bonus he might give to us.

I read in 1 Corinthians 12:27–30:

> Now you are the body of Christ, and each one of you is a part of it. And in the church God has appointed first of all apostles, second prophets, third teachers, then workers of miracles, also those having gifts of healing, those able to help others, those with gifts of administration, and those speaking in different kinds of tongues. Are all apostles? Are all prophets? Are all teachers? Do all work miracles? Do all have gifts of healing? Do all speak in tongues? Do all interpret?

In other words, none of us receives all of the gifts.

Some time ago I was visiting a minister friend and we were discussing the "problems" of the Charismatic movement. He said something that astonished me: "Ed, I have that gift." I said, "You do?" It blew my mind.

Then he said this to me: "You know I'd always understood why a person might want to have the gift of healing. I've understood that—as well as the gift of discernment, the gift of prophecy—but I could never understand how there could be any practical use for this gift of tongues.

"Ed, you know a baby has needs and feelings that it cannot express," he continued. "You and I are like that. We have needs and feelings we cannot express and the Holy Spirit takes those and releases them. For me, glossolalia is a prayer language."

If that is your experience, I affirm you.

There is a new tongue that is a necessary evidence to the Spirit-filled life. That's the tongue of kindness, the tongue of truth, the tongue of witness, the tongue of encouragement, and I want that tongue, don't you?

They left Pentecost with the shackles of fear struck away from them. What do you think is the evidence of a Spirit-filled church? Miracles? I believe in miracles. I *am* a miracle. However, that is not the evidence of a Spirit-filled church. What is it? Waving your hands? I'm glad in the United Methodist Church if we want to wave our hands we can. Sometimes I do. But that is not the evidence of a Spirit-filled church.

What's the evidence—singing Scripture choruses? I like to sing them—don't you? But that's not necessarily the evidence of a Spirit-filled church. So what is it? I'll tell you what it is— outreach, missions, evangelism, generosity. What happened on the day of Pentecost? Three thousand people were converted; turn a page, five thousand were converted; turn another page, great multitudes were converted. They shared what they had. They gave all. That is what we need today. Churches that are generous, churches that are evangelizing, churches that are concerned for the souls of men and women. This is the evidence of a Spirit-filled church.

Before Pentecost Jesus was a memory—after Pentecost he was a presence. I am afraid for many people Jesus is just a historical figure that they reverence, but he can be their contemporary. He can be their friend. He can be a presence, a reality, a power in their life.

I was in San Francisco attending the National Council on Evangelism of the United Methodist Church. We were at the Mark Hopkins Hotel on the top of Knob Hill. We were sitting around convincing the convinced. I've gone to those meetings for years, and we don't witness to anybody but fellow Christians. I announced that I was going to have a street service. I asked people to meet me out in front of the hotel that afternoon. I thought three or four would meet me. There must have been a hundred. We marched down Knob Hill singing "Onward Christian Soldiers" and "Amazing Grace," and concluded in front of Glide Church where we had a street service. Old Dr. J. C.

McPheeters, my spiritual father, was with us. When he got down on his knees you could hear him praying for a mile. I preached. Later that night we were down on Market Street. It was at the height of the hippie movement. I walked up to one young hippie and asked, "How long have you been in San Francisco?" He replied, "About two weeks." I said, "I was in San Francisco many years ago and I met Jesus Christ." He earnestly asked if I'd really met Jesus Christ. I said, "I really met him and he changed my life." The young man said, "I guess it would change your life if you *really* met him."

At Pentecost these disciples really met him. Others recognized the disciples had been with Jesus. There was joy, there was freedom, there was cleansing from sin, there was holiness of life.

How to Be Filled with The Holy Spirit

How shall we be filled with the Holy Spirit? Is your heart hungry? Would you like the fullness of God in your life? Anything short of the Spirit-filled life is less than God's plan for you. The question is not how much of the Spirit do you have but rather how much of you does the Spirit have. Being filled by the Spirit is not optional. It is necessary if we are going to have the abundant life.

I have noticed in the book of Acts the regularity of the *ir-regularity* of the Holy Spirit. I used to think I had it all worked out. There was one work of grace, and there was a second work of grace. There was justification and then there was sanctification. Then I heard about the Roman Catholics getting religion. Then I heard about "God's frozen people," the Presbyterians. They were getting religion. I thought, "It's not supposed to work that way." It comes to Methodists at a camp meeting, I thought at one time. Now everybody is getting religion. And I found that you cannot put God in a straitjacket. Your experience may be emotional and someone else's may not. You may cry and others do not. Others do not have to have the same kind of experience that you have. You cannot domesticate the Holy Spirit.

I was visiting with another Methodist preacher. We were talking about the great movement of the Spirit across the church today. He said, "Ed, it's all right if it doesn't get out of control." I thought, that is the problem. We have been trying to control the Spirit rather than allowing the Holy Spirit to control us.

To be Spirit-filled is not to be abnormal. It's not to be a fanatic, but instead it is becoming a whole person. The grace of God enables you to become what you ought to be and what you want to be.

There are some things that we will have in common if we are to be filled with the Spirit. One is, confession and repentance. Forsaking every known sin in one's life, giving all of ourselves that we know to all of God that we understand at that moment. Ask this question, "Who is ruling my life—Christ or self?" Then yield your life as fully as you know how at that moment. You'll know something else next week. And then claim by faith the promise of the Father. Remember it is not feeling we are trusting. It is Christ and the Holy Spirit that we are trusting. Claim the promise. Go forth rejoicing.

I want to give you my testimony. I was converted when I was 19. When I was a young student pastor 22 years of age, I read a magazine one day that told about the Spirit-filled life. I got on my knees and I surrendered everything to God. I felt a deep burning—a cleansing within. I got up from my knees and went to my church and testified that night as to what God had done. I had been Spirit-filled. The Lord blessed me tremendously. We had great revivals, my reputation grew and I was appointed to big churches and still bigger churches. People were saying, "You know you are good." I agreed with them. I thought some day I might be a bishop. And sometime down the line when I was climbing the ladder I lost the victory. I lost the joy. I was tempted to quit.

In 1971 I was in India. I always looked down on people who got sick on mission trips, but there I was in a hot, dirty, mosquito-infested hotel room in Bangalore, India, very ill. I was discouraged. I wondered why in the world I was in that place. I thought, "My children could die and I wouldn't even know it." I had never been so low.

In that moment I said to my wife, "Martha, I've always believed in the Spirit-filled life and God's sanctifying grace but it is just a doctrine. It is not real in my life." I asked her to pray for me. She put her hands on my head and prayed. As she prayed I yielded and the switchboard clicked in heaven. I didn't speak in tongues, I didn't have an emotional experience, but when I returned to the States I knew I was a new man. I had greater love, temptation did not have the same attraction, there was a new power in my life. My children can tell you that from that day to now I've been a different person. I haven't always been all I wanted to be, but I've never been what I was. It's the pivotal experience of my Christian life.

God wants to bless you, God wants to fill you, God wants to meet your need and he will do so if you yield.

Holy Spirit of the living God, descend on us we pray. Holy Spirit of the living God, speak to us this day. You promised that those who hunger and thirst for righteousness shall be satisfied. We hunger, we are thirsty for more of you. Fill us, bless us in Jesus' name.

Notes

1 Billy Graham, *The Holy Spirit* (Dallas: Word Books), p. 11.

2 Ibid.

3 "Holy, Holy, Holy."

4 Helen Smith Shoemaker, *I Stand By the Door; the Life of Sam Shoemaker* (New York: Harper & Row, 1967), p. xi.

5 For a complete account of Sangster's life, see Paul Sangster, *Dr. Sangster* (London: Epworth Press, 1962).